SUCCEEDING

With

Struggling Students

SUCCEEDING

With

Struggling Students

A PLANNING RESOURCE FOR RAISING ACHIEVEMENT

MARTI RICHARDSON   Foreword by *MAX THOMPSON*

CORWIN PRESS
A SAGE Publications Company
Thousand Oaks, CA 91320

KH

For information:

Corwin Press
A Sage Publications Company
2455 Teller Road
Thousand Oaks, California 91320
www.corwinpress.com

Sage Publications Ltd.
1 Oliver's Yard
55 City Road
London EC1Y 1SP
United Kingdom

Sage Publications India Pvt. Ltd.
B-42, Panchsheel Enclave
Post Box 4109
New Delhi 110 017 India

Printed in the United States of America.

Library of Congress Cataloging-in-Publication Data

Richardson, Marti.
  Succeeding with struggling students: A planning resource for raising achievement / Marti Richardson.
       p. cm.
Includes bibliographical references and index.
ISBN 1-4129-4462-7 or 978-1-412916-86-8 (cloth)
ISBN 1-4129-4463-5 or 978-1-412916-87-5 (pbk.)
    1. Learning disabled children—Education—United States.
2. Academic achievement—United States. I. Title.
LC4705.R52 2007
371.9—dc22   2006014863

This book is printed on acid-free paper.

06   07   08   09   10   10   9   8   7   6   5   4   3   2   1

Acquisitions Editor:	Jean Ward
Editorial Assistant:	Jordan Barbakow
Production Editor:	Diane S. Foster
Copy Editor:	Bill Bowers
Typesetter:	C&M Digitals (P) Ltd.
Proofreader:	Andrea Martin
Indexer:	Kathy Paparchontis
Cover Designer:	Michael Dubowe
Graphic Designer:	Lisa Miller

12\5\06

Contents

List of Figures

List of Worksheets: Resource Section

Foreword

Whether you argue vehemently against the regulations and talk incessantly about the lack of funding for certain provisions of No Child Left Behind, or you think it is the best federal or state educational framework ever enacted, or you are sitting back with a wait-and-see approach, most of us agree on the premise of the title. Let's teach *all* kids. Let's make sure no child is ignored or forgotten. Let's make sure *all* children learn and achieve to high standards. While many consider that an unrealistic goal, no one can argue that we have been very lax in even trying to attain it.

Today, schools and districts are working harder than ever in trying to meet that goal. The concept that every child should have a year's worth of growth for each year in school has become a much discussed and adopted vision for many schools. Even while being challenged by scarce resources, unfunded mandates, community opinion, educational bureaucracies, and board politics, schools have been making significant gains in student achievement and learning. They are finding ways to actually do it!

Having seen the results of the Preview Learning Program (PLP), I would indeed consider it a revolutionary innovation (see Chapter 2). I have seen first-hand how the development of a PLP using the planning model described in this book moved a school district to previously unheard-of student success. I am honored to write the foreword to this book because I have observed the passion and intelligence that Marti Richardson brings to the goal of *all children can learn and achieve.* Not only does her book offer the strategy (Preview Learning) for attaining that goal, but the book also offers a very specific framework and model for others to apply in developing their own revolutionary innovations.

This concept of Preview Learning does seem to be revolutionary. We have not lacked for possible solutions to the goal of educating all students. However, when it came to providing learning support for all of our economically disadvantaged students, or our students with disabilities, or our English Language Learners, we seem to have developed tunnel vision for the remedial process. "Wait until they fail and then try to remediate" has been the mantra for decades. We practiced remediation even in the face of overwhelming data showing that for every year in a remedial setting, students fall further below grade level. If a student is behind, is below grade level in achievement, how can we "catch that student up" to grade level by going backwards in the curriculum?

Marti Richardson presents excellent theories and powerful research for the planning model and the PLP strategy. However, I think a particular strength of the book is her commonsense approach, which enables the reader to really understand the model's framework. The book offers real-life examples and models for the reader on each component. This excellent scaffolding facilitates the reader's learning and implementation of the model.

I think the challenge to you, the reader, is to find the inspiration to use this model to find other revolutionary innovations such as the PLP; to find other strategies that ensure *all* students a year's worth of growth for every year in school. This model is added to the large and growing body of successful strategies that reinforce the twenty-first century core belief for American public education—the belief that all children can learn.

—Max Thompson

Preface

Today's weakness can be tomorrow's strength:
today's crisis, tomorrow's crown.

THE GENESIS OF THE BOOK

Underachieving students live in our midst. We see many of them at the grocery store, watch them play as we drive down the street, notice them hanging out with their friends at the local deli, and teach them when they arrive at our educational door. Their lack of attainment may be due to one single factor, but often it is a combination of many. In the elementary years, their inability to keep up with their peers may exhibit itself in phonological disorders—to name only one possibility—that create early reading problems. In the later years of their educational journey, many underachieving students simply drop out of school.

National statistics present the demographic scope of the problem. The same data do not tell of the human cost or the painful battle that these students face. To alleviate the growing problem, educational professionals have explored a variety of strategies. Some are designed for remediation, others for accommodation. Student reading skills have attracted the most attention for this subgroup, because reading lays the foundation for a successful future and because the numbers of students having trouble are increasing.

As a classroom teacher, I always had an extra passion for helping the child achieve who was performing below the expected level as indicated by tests of intelligence or aptitude. In a staff development supervisory position, I saw countless teachers match, or surpass, my level of passion as they struggled to find a way to connect with the underachiever with normal intelligence. The teachers and I wondered where academic achievement for each of our students had derailed from the forward movement on the track of learning. Our testing data supported the student's potential to learn, but acquiring knowledge was not demonstrated on test scores or in day-to-day gains in the classroom. To attack the problem, each of us used remedial curriculum materials prescribed for the grade level and even alternated instructional strategies to match each individual's unique situation. Because of a dedicated effort to find an approach that works, the students had some measure of attainment, but they never met grade-level expectations.

In this arena of personal concern, two things happened for me in a short period of time that made a major impact on my thinking. In the first event,

I was privileged to hear Max Thompson speak on learning-focused schools at a state supervisory study council. My short summary of his encouraging remarks includes three important ideas:

- Being behind grade level does not automatically rule out the possibility of making progress.
- There are remedies to help the student in the achievement gap become efficient and successful.
- Developing skills in poor readers takes more time, because they develop in a different way.

When I heard Thompson say, "Remediation doesn't work because the student never has the opportunity to catch up," something registered in my brain and resonated within my soul. How simple, yet profound! If a student works only on what he missed, he is destined to fall farther behind in school each year. This phenomenon must be changed! I, therefore, made a vow to spearhead some kind of program that would enable almost *every student* in my local system to read well and to understand grade-appropriate material by the end of elementary school.

Within a couple of weeks, the second thing happened that moved me to action. I was participating in a discussion with several experienced staff developers at a group meeting of the National Staff Development Council. The topic was ways to achieve the goal of all teachers in all schools experiencing high-quality professional learning on a daily basis. The executive director of the organization, Dennis Sparks, issued a challenge to each person sitting around the table. His request was for each of us to develop and implement a *Theory of Action* in our own work in order to set a model of how to reach the goal. His premise was that if the people with knowledge about and experience with staff development can make a difference in daily learning for students and educators, it might be assumed that others can do the same. I bought into the challenge because it made sense to me. In fact, the self-selected assignment turned into a passion.

A FRESH APPROACH TO THINKING

Having my thinking altered and my actions channeled, I was motivated to develop a plan that would help each child in my circle of influence achieve victory by learning to read. The plan was developed and implemented at the system level. It resulted in the exploration of a lab-based staff development concept that focused on both student and staff learning. The targeted student population was low-achieving children with IQ within the normal range. Working with a dedicated team of educators, we developed a program that includes new and appropriate curriculum coupled with suitable instructional strategies. A fresh process for teacher selection was written, and a staff development program designed that integrates multiple models of professional development and incorporates all the best strategies that we know to work that support educator learning.

The overarching concept of the program revolves around the idea presented by Max Thompson. The concept is called *Preview Learning* as opposed to the deficit/remediation model. It is an intervention for closing the achievement gap by focusing on teaching more, not less. Low achievers are given a preview of what they will learn, much like what they see when they go to the movies and get a preview of the "coming attractions." Low-achieving students are actually "presented" the information before others, but only in an introductory way. The preview focuses on a prioritized curriculum of state-standardized, grade-level essential skills. The student receives manageable bits of information before he is taught the same skill in a regular class. The teachers learn together, in a lab-based approach, how to "make it all happen." Briefly stated, the student is introduced to a skill or concept early, so that he can attain mastery more easily when he meets the same material in class. This is highly motivational for both students and teachers.

The complete design—along with tools for implementing the program, either partially or in its entirety—is the subject of this book. Each chapter may be used independently or as part of a larger whole. The book is written about an elementary program and focuses on the journey of one specific student whom I have named William. He is a fictional character, but he represents many students like him who face the same problems. One caution here to you, the reader: Do not let the focus on the elementary level blind you to a process that is applicable to any grade level, subject area, or planning endeavor. The material in this book can enhance decision making for school district personnel, staff developers, school and district administrators, district and school planners, special help teachers (i.e., reading assistants), literacy coaches, teacher leaders, and community leaders who face the task of implementing change and developing actions that require staff development at any level. The presentation of research-based, worthwhile information, detailed sample documents, end-of-chapter templates, and a complete resource section reflect practical considerations that will serve the needs of each of these audiences. The book is *not* a rehash of what is available commercially for the school year with a different name. It *is* a book that will inform your thinking, provide for you a scaffold between learning and action, and give you tools that you need to adapt the process from print to plan.

RESULTS

The Preview Learning Program (PLP) has resulted in documented improvement for the participants, who are continuing to learn and achieve. Teacher evaluation reports indicate that more effective instruction is taking place, even in the regular classrooms of PLP staff members. Chapter 7 provides an in-depth look into the evaluation framework, and Appendix A presents the results from year one of a PLP. The evidence of increased learning for both students and educators has been collected through questionnaires, surveys, tests, and existing databases, along with observations, interviews, and focus questions. The feedback was good. Children are learning now who have never before experienced that wonderful feeling that learning brings in a structured setting like school!

A SEQUENTIAL MODEL FOR PROGRAM PLANNING: ORGANIZATION AND CONTENT

This book is designed to be a practical manual for providing answers to a mosaic of powerful questions that educators continually struggle to answer: How can we ensure that all students can learn? What curriculum should be in place for the underachiever? How can we provide congruence between curriculum and brain-based instructional strategies? What instructional strategies work best for students who are behind their peers in learning? How can we develop standards-based professional growth activities that ensure daily high-quality learning for all? How can we recruit and select the most effective educators? What and how do we assess on a regular basis to ensure desired results? A new, fresh approach is presented here in a detailed model on how to answer these questions to get broader options for erasing the failure of students who are not yet mastering grade-level objectives.

The cornerstone of the book is William. Throughout the book, his reader-friendly case study, and the model that his district developed to ensure his learning, integrate the focus of eliminating the achievement gap. The definition of "achievement gap" is presented early in the book, and sound principles of learning support a presentation of relevant domains. All of the information couples with a composite set of strategies that will challenge each of us to rethink our actions in a revolutionary way. A quick look at the organization of the book and an overview of each chapter's contents will focus us on how to use the material in any subject area or across grade levels. The planning template that is presented at the end of each chapter will facilitate your planning, challenge you to act on the material presented, and make the chapter-specific information come to life for you as you build a plan for moving forward.

Chapter 1 presents William. You will identify with William, because everyone has met a William. The lead character may represent to you a William who is either male or female, has another name, belongs to a different ethnic group, lives geographically in another place, or is in a different subgroup. He is special to the story because he is trapped in the achievement gap and, under normal circumstances, has no apparent way out. Research-based information explains the achievement gap to us, and a review of data in William's system sets the stage for each chapter that follows.

Chapter 2 explores three concepts, intricately interwoven with the subject matter, to provide a rationale for the type of thinking that is necessary to develop an innovative and creative program. Examples and strategies for facilitating creative thinking help scaffold your learning along a continuum from background knowledge to informed decision making.

Chapter 3 focuses on a hiring IQ and provides a process for selecting *effective* teachers. The critical question, "What results do I want?" drives the process. Directions for implementing the process are complete, and commonsense tools are included to help program planners move from highly qualified teachers to effectiveness in teaching.

Chapter 4 reduces a complex curriculum building process to its most common denominator. Principles of learning support the foundation and rationale for the model presented here. Powerful questions, strategically selected essential skills, and unique strategies provide resources that are important to the curriculum planning process.

The acquisition lesson is the linchpin of **Chapter** 5. Sample lessons illustrate the design of the acquisition lesson, and sample lessons for four different literacy strands are presented as models. The acquisition lesson is important because it contributes to instruction that is skill-specific and enables low achievers to become engaged in their own learning in a meaningful and productive way.

High-quality professional learning produces complex, intelligent behavior. Conversely, when teachers are not strengthened through significant staff development they may develop instructional atrophy! The material in each chapter of the book has the potential to be used as a standalone for selective professional development activities, but **Chapter 6** is different because it stresses that professional development of teachers is the key to bridging the student's gap in achievement! The title of the chapter speaks to its focus. A well-designed professional development model is embedded in a lab-based learning design. The various designs of staff development are examined, and a comprehensive timetable, showing each component of the design used in the PLP, is presented for easy review.

Qualitative and quantitative measures are promoted in the evaluation process found in **Chapter 7**. Formative and summative evaluations are discussed, and ways to expand the program into a different arena are examined. The evaluation plan is a valuable model for the assessment of any program.

Chapter 8 wraps up the story of William and explains his achievement in the PLP. A final challenge is issued here, urging each of us to confront the urgent problem of the achievement gap with bold and courageous strategies. These strategies are available in this book to all who will spend the time necessary to read the material, get a good grasp on the concepts, and then act decisively and aggressively on the home front to apply the new learning. Yes, the processes of developing and refining will take time, expertise, and effort. However, they can be the catalyst that helps the students who are lost in the cycle of failure emerge from the abyss of underachieving to a new day of achieving.

Acknowledgments

This compilation of material evolved into a book through the support and assistance of many people. The hero of the book is William, but there are many heroes in my life who contributed in some way to the development and completion of this project. I appreciate each of them.

A special thank-you is extended to Don Richardson for his constant support, encouragement, and patience. He is the wind beneath my wings. Gratitude is expressed to Donna, Eddie, and Susan for their loving hearts, willingness to help in a multitude of ways, and for lending their technical support and sharing their computer expertise. I also acknowledge Laura Kay, Paul, and Matthew, who are shining examples of skilled readers. They brighten my day and have traits that I wish for children the world over: compassion, awareness, gratitude, and curiosity, along with knowledge and integrity that grows as they mature and develop.

My appreciation is extended to Max Thompson, who expanded my knowledge base about learning-focused schools and inspired my thinking about preview learning. He honors me by writing the foreword for this book. I am grateful for Dennis Sparks and his provocative leadership on the national staff development stage and for his unique call to action for high-quality daily learning for all. For his support of this book I am especially grateful.

A special thank-you goes to the design, implementation, and support teams in the Knox County Schools. Excellence in this program was achieved because of the dedication, shared expertise, perseverance, and concern for underachieving children that was in evidence in the work of many: Sarah Simpson (now deceased), LaNoka Rhodes, Zulette Melnick, Sonja Armstrong, Fran Thomforde, Mike Winstead, Barbara Clark, Sue Boyer, Theresa Wishart, Laura Boring, Beverly Hutchinson, Deanna Heflin, Mary Lynn Coyne, Jennifer Thomas, Becky Kidd, Brandy Hall, and Andrea Russell.

Jean Ward, my editor, has provided support, expertise, and valuable suggestions throughout the development of this material. Thank you, Jean, for excellence and for providing me a way, through this book, to enter the public conversation about student attainment and effective teaching. Appreciation is expressed also to Douglas Rife and the Corwin Press staff for their cooperation and assistance.

To all the teachers and administrators who facilitated the learning process in the Preview Learning Program, your acknowledgment is found within each of you, because you have brought joy and new hope to the hearts and minds of the many children you encountered daily during the four weeks of the program and beyond into the regular school year.

About the Author

Marti Richardson is a leader in the field of staff development. At the international level, she has led workshops on instructional strategies and worked with teacher study groups in multiple countries in Europe and the South Pacific. Nationally, she has been a conference presenter for the National Staff Development Council (NSDC), the Association for Supervision and Curriculum Development (ASCD), the Mid-South Educational Research Association (MSERA), Phi Delta Kappa, and others. She was host chair for an annual conference of the NSDC and served as president of the same organization during one year of her six-year terms on the NSDC board of trustees. At the state level, she was a founding member of the Tennessee Staff Development Council (TSDC). A former president of the TSDC, she is currently serving as its executive director. She has served as a director of other statewide training programs, organized state conferences and institutes, and actively worked on numerous task forces and boards. Her 17 years as a classroom teacher at the local level gave her a working knowledge of classroom needs that validated her later roles as teacher center director, staff development supervisor, and supervisor of extended learning programs. In-system, and at the state and national levels, she has served as a trainer, facilitator, coach, and mentor.

Her expertise in the areas of strategic planning, curriculum development, instructional strategies, and staff development has led to the writing of numerous curriculum materials, trainer-of-trainer modules, brochures, and booklets. Her informative columns have been published in the *Journal of Staff Development*. Marti is also credited in numerous other authors' books, manuscripts, critiques, and book reviews.

Her professional goal is to facilitate enhanced learning for adults and children. All of her collaborations, networking, inquiry, and innovative thinking and planning have been focused on opening every mind in her circle of influence to the limitless possibilities for growth and development.

This book is dedicated to my mother, Jewel Taylor, who was my first and best teacher. During her years as a classroom teacher, she enriched the lives of hundreds of children on a daily basis by opening the door to learning in a differentiated way.

Laying the Foundation

Identifying Needs

*The needs of one child
often reflect a larger need
for other children in the nation.*

MEET WILLIAM

William has an IQ of 100, loves to be around his friends and just "hang out," and is a basketball fan during basketball season and a fan of football when that season arrives. Sports are important to him. Both of his parents work outside the home to give him and his brother and sister the advantages they never had. His teachers say that he is shy in class and has a hard time achieving. When the school day is over he becomes more outgoing and social.

Let's peep in on William in class on a day that is special for him. The day is special because he has been chosen to be the class "Leader for the Day." As we watch, he has a lift in his step and appears motivated as he walks to the front of the line to lead the group to music class. Later in the day he exhibits pure joy when he is captain of the kickball team at outside playtime. His classmates respect his athletic ability while he is on the playground. We see a different William, however, when the students are back in the classroom working on academics. He lacks excitement, and his peers tend to ignore him.

During reading class, William has a story about whales. William whispers to the boy beside him that he watches programs about whales on cable TV. He seems interested in the topic. The lesson begins with his teacher directing the students to begin reading the story silently after she has given a brief overview about what whales look like and where they live. She tells them in her overview that the story for the day is about a large humpback whale, named Willie, who is worried because he does not have as much hair today as he had a month ago, or even last week. William begins to read as directed, but as William looks at his book, it is apparent to us, the unseen observers, that he is having difficulty reading the story. He makes a grimacing movement with his mouth when he comes to a word that isn't part of his background knowledge. We surmise that he doesn't have the necessary skills to decode the strange words. By the time William struggles through the first page, he gives up "reading" and just pretends to be completing his assignment. As we look at William from our unseen vantage point, it appears to us that he has developed a real skill in looking at a page and making it look to others as if he is on task.

The class discusses the story, but William does not participate. The teacher must know that he didn't read anything, because she does not call on him to answer any of the comprehension questions. The rest of the students don't acknowledge that William is there, either. As we look in on our scene, we get the idea that this is the norm for William, the class, and the teacher when group participation is expected.

Today, William fell behind the majority of the children in his class in skill attainment. The next day's lesson will probably be more of the same, meaning that William will continue to accumulate days where he falls farther and farther behind in his academic achievement. He may be two weeks behind now, or he may be as much as a year behind—or even more—in the continuum of skills for his grade level. The degree to which he is behind will depend on the number of days that he has been in school during the current school year and when the instruction that he received in previous years began to be a mismatch for his instructional level and style of learning. William isn't aware that he is not achieving at the desired level of learning. All he knows is that he is glad when it is time to go home at the end of the school day. Sitting in the classroom is no fun at all!

Educators with any experience have seen a William. He may be either gender or have another name, belong to a different ethnic group, live in another place, or be in a different socioeconomic group. Whatever the subgroup, the problem for all the Williams is the same. They are a part of a vacuum, or gap, which exists between what should be learned, based on grade-level standards, and what is actually learned. All of our Williams are students trapped in the *achievement gap!*

THE ACHIEVEMENT GAP

The achievement gap means different things to different people. It is given, a definition in a variety of resources, including the Education Trust, North Central Regional Educational Laboratory (NCREL), the Center on Education Policy, and the Educational Research Service (ERS). The Policy and Program Service addresses the topic specifically in their Longitudinal Assessment of

Comprehensive School Reform (CSR). Educational journals such as *Phi Delta Kappan*, the *Journal of Staff Development*, and *Educational Leadership* have published numerous articles on the achievement gap. Entire conferences have been organized around the topic in an effort to help educators understand the broader implications of the concept, and task forces have gathered to study the disparities in achievement for various subgroups.

One definition for the achievement gap that is heard most frequently refers to "the achievement level of poor, minority students as a group, who score lower in student achievement measures than do middle-class, nonminority students" (ERS, 2001). There is another school of thought (Burkhardt, 2002) that holds that the achievement gap isn't restricted to just poor and minority students. This definition incorporates the concept that the gap cuts across income and geography and includes middle-income and upper-income students in suburban schools who are found to have deficits in learning.

The definition preferred here maintains that the achievement gap is primarily a problem of attainment—not of race, ethnicity, or innate ability. There are many poor and minority students who perform at high levels. As a matter of fact, all subgroups have a full range of achievement from high to low. The No Child Left Behind Act of 2001 (NCLB Act) acknowledges this definition, addresses the substandard performance of all children, and then gives educators a charge to erase the achievement gap. If the gap is in the urban community, academic attainment must increase. If the area is suburban or rural, standards must be met. No group is to be excluded. This includes socioeconomically disadvantaged and culturally diverse students.

The gap in achievement among different groups of students that ushered in the twenty-first century (Haycock, 2001a) must be eliminated. We knew how to narrow the gap during the 1970s and 1980s. We should be able to do it now. The Williams whom we know wouldn't be having the attainment problem they have now if schools and districts would close their knowing-and-doing gap in curriculum and instruction, align their policies and practices with research on what works (Marzano, 2004), and address substandard performance of all students, regardless of race, gender, or geography. It would make no difference that our William lives in an area of the city that has been neglected for a number of years and is now undergoing urban renewal. The fact that he is a regular education student without an attendance deficit should be more important to his status than the fact that he falls behind on a daily basis. The slippery slope of failure that currently profiles William's potential should be eliminated and replaced with incremental steps to academic success.

William is an indicator of the need for a deep change at many levels. The level closest to him is the district where his school is located. Let's examine some data from the district and use this information to expand our understanding of William's need.

WILLIAM'S DISTRICT

To understand if there is an achievement gap in William's district, it will be easier—for the purposes of our discussion—to focus on the core subject of

Figure 1.1   William's District

District Totals	Number	Percent
Number of Schools	90 51 Elementary 14 Middle 13 High School 12 Special Education	
Grades Served	K–12	
Number of Students K–12	53,000	
• White	44,997	85.0%
• African-American	6,500	12.2%
• Hispanic	900	1.7%
• Asian	502	0.9%
• Native American	88	0.2%
• Pacific Islander	13	0.02%
Economically Disadvantaged	17,575	33.0%

reading. This is not done to intentionally exclude other core subjects. Rather, we focus on reading because our earlier observation of William was, in part, during his reading class. By choosing to look only at reading, we will have a continuity in our thinking as we analyze the data at the local level.

A few numbers will begin our cursory examination of the district's general data. These numbers may be seen in Figure 1.1.

William's district uses a variety of instruments to measure students' academic growth, including nationally normed achievement tests and several local assessments, such as districtwide tests for reading. As a system, the district consistently scores above state and national averages. In fact, it is the highest-performing large system in its state; however, a disaggregation of the data reveals a problem that has not previously been noticed.

There are 2,935 students systemwide who read in the first quartile in grades 2–5, the only elementary grades tested in William's district. The district includes 51 elementary schools, and 1,345 of the 2,935 students, or 46 percent, attend one of the 10 inner-city schools. That is almost one-half of the district's reading problems in only 20 percent of the schools. Seventy-six percent of the 1,345 students are economically disadvantaged, and all ten of the inner-city schools receive Title I funds. The number of African-American students in the lowest quartile in reading in those schools is 1,785 (61 percent), with Hispanics numbering 416. William attends one of these schools.

Given the data to review, the district's administrators, specialists, and a data team realize that the information they have been hearing and reading about the achievement gap is more than an array of factors and findings that happen in other places. The data take on a new meaning as they speak to them from the paper in their hands. The educators note also that there is reason to be concerned about the learning in the remaining 41 schools. Their data indicate that they are affected, too. The data tell us that there are 1,590 (54 percent) students attending the 41 schools in the rest of the district who read in the lowest quartile, with an average of 38 students per school and nine students per grade. These students will need an intervention to meet their needs. William's district will not ignore the needs of the inner-city youngsters, and will not ignore the lack of attainment of the students in the lowest quartile in the rural and suburban areas.

ADDRESSING THE PROBLEM

Armed with new information, the district's leaders acknowledge that there is a severe achievement gap, greater in some schools than in others, and they make a commitment to "erase the failure" of these youngsters. The administrative team knows that there is expertise within the district to develop a plan to significantly reduce, or even eliminate, the deficit that is found in this stubborn gap. With intentionality, they decide to plan, implement, and evaluate all the elements that research suggests are necessary to impact an area of need.

The information that follows in this book will guide you through the development of the plan, with the express purpose of giving you a tool to use if you have a similar need. The strategies within each chapter can also provide information to support the chapter's focus in an area of need other than the achievement gap. For example, Chapter 3, "Selecting Educators," includes a dynamic plan for the selection process. That plan is appropriate for any area in education, not just for selecting personnel to work in a program that addresses the achievement gap. At the end of each chapter is a template for you to use reflectively to analyze your system's needs and develop an action plan. It is expected that this book will inform your thinking and give you the tools that you need to adapt, not adopt (Thompson, 2005) strategies that will bridge the achievement gap and enhance learning opportunities for students in your circle of influence.

I have come to believe that every child can learn the next thing that follows the last thing they learned. This acquisition of learning by all students can happen with proper assessment, appropriate cognitive strategies, effective instruction, targeted curriculum, quality professional learning, and a passion to see others succeed. The learning is, above all, about making a difference in the life chances for all students, including the disadvantaged (Fullan, 1999). There is, therefore, an innovation described in this book that will make it possible for you to tackle the mandate of achieving parity in achievement across diverse groups of students. There is a structure built into the model to help bring order out of the chaos of the achievement gap. There are also tables, charts, and worksheets to support you in your nonlinear journey as you acquire new knowledge and develop new strategies to address an old problem. The model is simple in its presentation but complex in the results that it brings. Read it. Study it. Then find a team in your system to make the model live for you. You owe it to the learners in your system.

MAKING IT "LIVE" FOR YOU: A PLANNING TEMPLATE

1. Complete the following sentence stems:
   - The articles or books that I have read about the achievement gap include . . .
   - The Web sites that I have found with relevant information include . . .
   - My knowledge of the topic that I already have includes . . .
   - The definition of the achievement gap that will be used in my district is . . .

2. Complete Worksheet 1.1 (see page 174 in the Resources) with general information about your district.

3. Complete Worksheet 1.2 (see page 175 in the Resources) with testing resources available in your district.

4. Complete Worksheet 1.3 (see page 176 in the Resources) with the testing data from your system.

5. Complete Worksheet 1.4 (see page 177 in the Resources) by doing a school-by-school analysis of the subgroups.

6. Complete Worksheet 1.5 (see page 178 in the Resources) with names of district administrators, subject-area specialists, and data specialists who can help plan the intervention strategy that will be used in your district.

7. Complete Worksheet 1.6 (see page 179 in the Resources) with questions that you have at this point in your deliberation.

8. Prioritize your next steps in Worksheet 1.7 (page 179 in the Resources).

2

Planning How
We Got There

*The significant problems we face
cannot be solved at the same level
at which we created them.*

—Albert Einstein

PAVING THE WAY:
PREPARING TO DEVELOP THE MODEL

Three concepts must be thoroughly understood and addressed at the beginning of the planning process for an innovation. Resolving the *how* of each will change the focus from defining the problem to doing something about it.

Concept One: Programming
must be addressed in a new way.

A unique approach is needed. The components currently being used in William's district to address remedial needs include pull-out activities, in-class assistance, and a special summer "catch-up" session. None of the three is effective as they are currently structured. The 2,935 students floundering in the achievement gap are a testimony to this fact.

Concept Two: A revolutionary, not evolutionary, approach must be identified.

The dictionary defines *revolution* as a "sudden, radical or complete change . . . a basic reorientation." It means changing direction. More of the same would be evolutionary. Adding more pull-out programs because you are dealing with larger numbers of children is evolutionary. Placing another in-class assistant with a teacher will not move any of the Williams forward in meaningful skill development; neither will it get the students far enough or fast enough for them to be at, or near, the same performance level as the majority of the students in their classes. The gap will remain! Having William attend a summer class for a mini-term of "review and recap" will produce minimal improvement that will not sustain itself. Therefore, the revolutionary approach needs to be a reengineered organizational structure, an innovation.

Innovation means *"putting new, high-value ideas into action"* (Dundon, 2005). Innovation and creativity are not interchangeable. Innovation is more than originality. An innovation includes four elements:

- Creativity—Combining a new idea with a mix of existing strategies or products
- Strategy—Finding options that are valuable for the situation
- Implementation—Setting the new idea into action
- Gain—Adding value

Changing direction means combining all four of these elements into a unified whole.

Concept Three: Both horizontal and vertical thinking will generate innovative ideas.

In a concept created by DeBono (1970) we learn that thinking must be both vertical (thinking within the known boundaries of knowledge) and horizontal (thinking beyond the known boundaries of knowledge) to get a progression of knowledge and expanded thinking. Vertical thinking is developmental *and* sequential thinking that gives an in-depth look into an idea. Horizontal thinking is creative, brings new ideas and thoughts, does not have to be sequential, and will provide important new areas for vertical development.

Chuck Frey, on his Web site Innovation Tools (www.innovationtools.com), says we should always begin the exploration of a new intervention with vertical thinking. The information found in the vertical thinking is basic information that lays the foundation for an intelligent or plausible breakthrough. Vertical thinking is evolutionary in nature. Examining ways that other districts have tackled similar challenges is an example of vertical thinking. Resources that will help in vertical thinking include online research, journal articles, and engaging in dialogue with other people who are knowledgeable about the topic of the innovation. Breakthrough thinking *may* result from vertical thinking alone, but that is rare.

To be productive, horizontal thinking should follow focused vertical think-ing and be integrated into the first-generation ideas. After that, horizontal thinking can be a vehicle to use to produce more unique ideas and give added energy to the group's planning. Creativity will be sparked when things are pushed in a new direction and new paradigms are sought. An educational example of horizontal thinking is offering youngsters who are lagging behind in academic growth an online tutorial that the school streams to homes via the Internet on a daily basis. A newer paradigm would be making the same tutor-ial live and interactive. This horizontal thinking is revolutionary.

DEVELOPING THE MODEL

As described previously, an effective innovation must be in place to help William—now! The need for change is great. The question that begs an answer at this point is, "How do I plan and frame the innovation with sound program theory?" McTighe and Wiggins (1999) alert us to the fact that this will be more difficult than it sounds by writing that *"design work is more than iterative; it is idiosyncratic."* That is why horizontal thinking is important! To the planners in William's district, the idiosyncratic nature of design work means that previ-ously developed planning models in their resource library may not fully meet the design needs for the innovation's starting point or sequence of activities. The modules may not even be aligned with the ideas that have been expressed during the creative thinking process. An idea, or a model, must still be identi-fied to address the unique and specific needs of the district.

An instructional task force (ITF) of qualified program development per-sonnel in William's district is, therefore, selected and charged with "designing an innovation which will be a constructive force for improved student learning and enhanced leadership and teaching practice." The group's assignment also includes defining the innovation and establishing the framework for the pro-gram. This means that the group will systematically work with program plan-ning and evaluation and develop all related components of the revolutionary course of action. In essence, the group will be the architects of the program and, as such, will develop the mural that will become the *big picture* of the inno-vation. The new picture and, more important, the process of creating the picture, will enable the district to create a work of art that will embody mean-ing for all low achievers in the district.

Making sense of complex issues surrounding the achievement gap will require the ITF to gather information. This will be accomplished through two strategies. The strategies, and the examples that give them life, follow.

Strategy One: Stimulate Creative Thinking

There are numerous strategies that may be used to jump-start idea genera-tion and gather information for both vertical and horizontal thinking. Three short examples are listed here because they were used successfully by the ITF in William's district to stimulate creative thinking. Note that each idea becomes

Form 2.1 Wisdom Storm (Vertical Thinking)

Things that I know about underachieving students include . . .

> ➤

> ➤

> ➤

> ➤

> ➤

> ➤

---

progressively more specific. The increased specificity allows planners to refine their thinking with each exercise.

Example One: Wisdom Storm (Vertical Thinking)

If working with a group, show Form 2.1 as a graphic. Have individuals think about their responses for 30 seconds before asking them to write as many words or short phrases as possible in three minutes. At the end of three minutes, request groups of four or five to combine their lists into a group list, with a group recorder making the composite list. Share each group's thinking with the larger group. A structured way to verbalize ideas to a group is through a "crack the whip" method. Simply stated, each group will give one idea in turn until all different thoughts have been shared. When all the ideas have been stated from a small group, it is appropriate for a group to pass and let the next small group proceed until all small groups have shared out. A complete list for the larger group should be compiled.

Example Two: Storytelling (Horizontal Thinking)

Storytelling is a good horizontal thinking strategy that may be used to promote dialogue and decide on an inventive and meaningful outcome.

Bring together enough people (no more than 50) so that seven to ten groups of five or six folks each can work together. By using several small groups, more ideas will be generated. Conversely, small groups need enough people to have a discussion. Telling a story that allows a large group to creatively explore solutions to problems through a structured format is the objective of the activity. The story will have three parts.

Story Part 1:

Who: Group facilitator

What facilitator says: "Once upon a time there was (a group of students who did not achieve academically)." *Facilitator provides a theme or problem area. The theme in William's district is shown above as an example.*

Story Part 2:

Who: Group facilitator

What facilitator says: "One day something spectacular happened for those low achievers. The district . . ."

Group members should brainstorm endings for the sentence. Insert new processes, strategies, or activities that contribute to the district finding a meaningful outcome. The description should be practical, yet imaginative, and tell how the challenge was resolved successfully. This part is horizontal thinking and should be carefully explored in a large group. If butcher paper and markers will help the group chart their thinking more creatively, they should be provided.

Story Part 3:

Who: Led by group facilitator; all participate

What is said: "This is how it turned out." _____

Each small group generates the ending of the story. Share out the story endings with the large group. Chart significant phrases from each story's finale. Discuss as appropriate.

All three strategies may be used deliberately to spur thinking and navigate through complex concepts. If time permits, use all three to have rich conversations that are developmental with results that are unique.

Strategy Two: Ask Powerful Questions

Powerful questions in program planning are questions that will contribute to the organization of domains, or manageable pieces, of the innovation. They are posed as "what-if" questions. What-if questions are often intriguing, can get folks in design out of a rut, and get creative juices flowing (Palus & Horth, 2002). When developed, the domains become lenses through which planners can simplify the complexity of the work and identify program components.

The domains that were identified in William's district are shown in Figure 2.2 (a–e) along with the initial what-if questions that the ITF generated. The questions are listed in the order in which they were randomly generated. They may be used as the basis for multiple discussions.

(*Text continues on page 17*)

Figure 2.2a   What-if Question (Standards, Curriculum)

Domain	What-if Question
Standards	. . . standards require new curricula?
	. . . new standards suggest that teachers will work more effectively if they work inter/intra grade level?
	. . . standards require new ways of assessing student learning?
	. . . standards require using results to change instruction when students aren't "getting it?"
	. . . standards require more time from some students than others?
Curriculum	. . . new curriculum is required for the innovation?
	. . . students are organized in new ways to provide them a different access to a new curriculum?
	. . . time is used differently to present curriculum to different types of students?
	. . . time is allocated differently to the content areas?
	. . . a curriculum framework is developed that will increase students' capacity to read fluently and with greater understanding?
	. . . a curriculum is developed to be presented in small steps in order to provide opportunity to practice after each step?
	. . . there are areas of the curriculum that are more specific to the needs of the low-achieving reader?
	. . . there are curriculum priorities that will affect student learning?
	. . . there are some specific skills that are essential to meet standards and others that are less important?
	. . . the curriculum is designed to assist students in organizing, storing, and retrieving knowledge?

Figure 2.2b   What-if Question (Instruction, Personnel)

Domain	What-if Question
Instruction	. . . instructional time is allocated differently?
	. . . we teach more, not less?
	. . . we use informational texts as an integral part of instruction?
	. . . we capture creative daily instructional strategies in an innovative model?
	. . . we teach the same thing at more than one site?
	. . . the daily schedule is one half-day for instruction of students?
	. . . we engage students in diversified learning activities 95 percent or more of the instructional time?
	. . . we incorporate structured dialogue between teacher and student?
	. . . some instructional strategies are more effective than others?
Personnel	. . . we find a procedure to hire the most qualified teachers to teach in the program?
	. . . we define qualifications that are desired in the teacher selection process?
	. . . there are instructional specialists available to coach and give feedback on instructional strategies?
	. . . we have key personnel in place to monitor, direct, and coordinate the program's activities?
	. . . we have adequate personnel at every site?
	. . . we have inadequate personnel at every site?

Figure 2.2c What-if Question (Personnel, Professional Development)

Domain	What-if Question
Personnel	. . . teachers don't want to participate in the innovation?
	. . . administrators are available at each site?
	. . . supervisors assist in program implementation?
	. . . the role of each educator category is formally defined in written form?
Professional Development	. . . the daily schedule includes one half-day for teaching and one half-day for professional growth?
	. . . there are changes in practice that will be necessary for teachers to be effective in teaching the low achieving student?
	. . . teachers need a change in knowledge, attitudes, skills, and behaviors to improve student achievement?
	. . . only professional development activities that will impact student achievement are included?
	. . . teachers get involved in collaboration?
	. . . teachers become part of a professional learning community?
	. . . teachers apply what they learn through the innovation to their classroom practice during the regular school year?
	. . . teachers work daily with each other on related student work?
	. . . teachers are invited to reflect on their work?
	. . . administrators, teachers, instructional specialists, and supervisors are asked to self-assess?
	. . . educators participating in the innovation are asked to write their assumptions about teaching?

Figure 2.2d   What-if Question (Assessment, Evaluation)

Domain	What-if Question
Assessment	. . . alternative strategies are used to assess student learning?
	. . . we document and communicate students' progress in learning?
	. . . we invite students to reflect on their work?
	. . . we need to validate the innovation to the veteran teachers in the district?
	. . . we report each student's progress to their base school?
	. . . resources are needed to effectively assess the innovation?
	. . . we assess each student's work on a daily basis?
	. . . we assess the curricular and instructional strategies that we develop?
Evaluation	. . . we build in a quality control method for planning the program?
	. . . we monitor instructional compliance of the program model?
	. . . check to see who the program did not reach?
	. . . the program has no impact on low achievers?
	. . . the program has an impact on low achievers?
	. . . we have a comprehensive evaluation plan to let us know if we met our goal?
	. . . we have resources available for the evaluation?

Figure 2.2e What-if Question (Administration, Other)

Domain	What-if Question
Administration	. . . we need multiple sites for delivery of services?
	. . . we need to provide food for the students?
	. . . transportation is required for the students?
	. . . funds are available from different sources? How will they be allocated and managed?
	. . . resources are already available in the district?
	. . . the innovation must be "sold" to the community, the administrators, and the policy-making body?
	. . . a communication plan is developed?
	. . . the innovation is successful?
Other	

Articulating the Model

Using the above strategies, a district can *name* or identify an intervention. Care is recommended at this stage, however. The Web site www.conservativefo rum.org quotes Peter Drucker, a United States management consultant, educator, and author of over 25 books about society, politics, and economics: "The greatest danger in times of turbulence is not the turbulence; it is to act with yesterday's logic" (Drucker, 2005). It is an earlier logic that is being played out in interventions that are currently in place in William's district. Three exercises are explained here that will continue to spur the horizontal thinking required to identify an intervention that will be specific to the system's identified need. *Each exercise is necessary to help a team or task force work smart on the right thing.*

Exercise One: Evaluative Thinking

There is a simple and effective management tool with wide application that can help guide decision making. It has become a popular equation for both personal and professional success. Called the 80/20 Principle, or Pareto Principle, it shows us how we can achieve more by concentrating on those areas that increase the possibility that we will accomplish the outcomes that we want to achieve. The 80/20 Principle says that 80 percent of the performance that we want to achieve will come out of 20 percent of what we are already doing. Examples of the 80/20 Principle include:

- Twenty percent of a meeting's duration results in 80 percent of its value.
- Twenty percent of the curriculum accounts for 80 percent of the essential skills and concepts.
- Eighty percent of the learning comes during 20 percent of the instruction.

Business and industry continually use this principle to improve quality— whether it is a product or a service. The Pareto Principle should be used more by educators!

In using the principle to direct us to the format of our innovation, questions will again be useful:

- What small thing are we already doing in the system that, if tweaked or reformatted, will let us effectively address our problem?
- What do the "what-if" questions lead us to investigate in the way of existing programming?
- What will allow us to teach more and not less to the low achiever?
- What is evolutionary that can be made revolutionary by focusing on the data gathered at the diagnostic stage?
- What intervention do we have in place that can accommodate the large numbers of students who have been identified as the target population?

Examining the in-system data on the success rate of the existing interventions will give us information. In William's district, the intervention that was identified as having the potential for a total makeover was *summer school*. The summer school program that is currently in place focuses on remediation. A review of student attendance shows that 20 percent of the students who enroll in the program complete the make-up work that drew them to the program in the first place. There are no data, however, to show that learning actually took place for any of the students. Mainly, the students put in their required seat time immediately following the end of the regular school year. Summer school appears to be a place where some "magic" of innovation will work!

Exercise Two: Fishbone Model

The Fishbone is used to brainstorm in a structured format. It will be effective in designing the summer program. An analysis tool that uses graphics, the Fishbone will give increased understanding of the anticipated framework and components for the new summer innovation in William's district. Use the Fishbone in the following way.

Fishbone: Step One. Define the problem.

The problem in the district is stated as, "What components are needed in the summer school in William's district that will help low achievers attain success and begin to catch up to the achievement level of their peers?" Figure 2.3 shows the Fishbone format, which states the problem graphically.

Figure 2.3   Fishbone (Define the Problem)

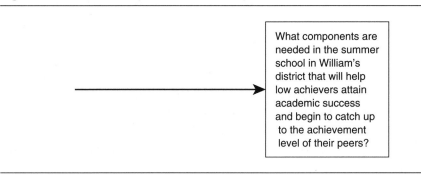

Fishbone: Step Two. Have preliminary brainstorming.

Identify the components that will help arrive at answers. The best solutions will usually be classified into one of the six "M" categories:

- **M**ethod
- **M**an
- **M**anagement
- **M**easurement
- **M**aterial
- **M**eans

The "M" categories are added to the Fishbone as indicated in Figure 2.4.

Figure 2.4 Fishbone ("M" Categories)

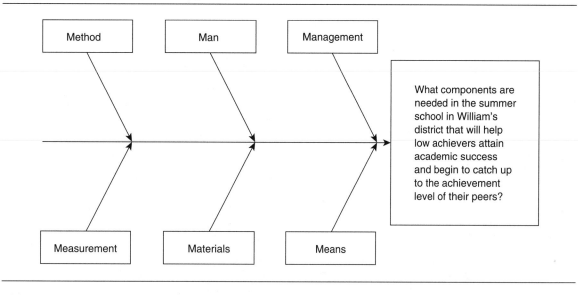

Fishbone: Step Three. Analyze each category.

Identify all possible components for each category. Be sure to consider what falls within the policy of the district. Place your considerations in "bonelets" within each category. Figure 2.5 shows all the ideas that were considered *workable* for the summer school for William's district.

The diagram can get very large and look crowded. A simple and neat-looking Fishbone, however, may indicate a need for more brainstorming to explore sufficient knowledge to address the problem.

Identifying the Specific Intervention

After you've completed all the components of the Fishbone, the intervention that will meet the district's needs may finally be identified. In William's district, the comprehensive analysis resulted in a definition of the intervention and included elements that would expand the program to give it more depth.

Definition: A Preview Learning Program (PLP) will teach more, not less, and:

- Be an intervention in the summer for students in the lower quartile of reading in Grades 1 through 5
- Have a skill-based, prioritized curriculum that will be offered during a four-week period just before school starts
- Include a lab-based staff development program in the afternoons where teachers focus on student learning
- Feature morning instructional sessions for students with a low student-teacher ratio, to include no more than eight students per teacher
- Utilize an instructional design
- Focus on formative and summative assessment as part of an evaluation design

This definition will enable the group to put the basic model of the PLP in place.

Figure 2.5   Fishbone (Categories and "Bonelets")

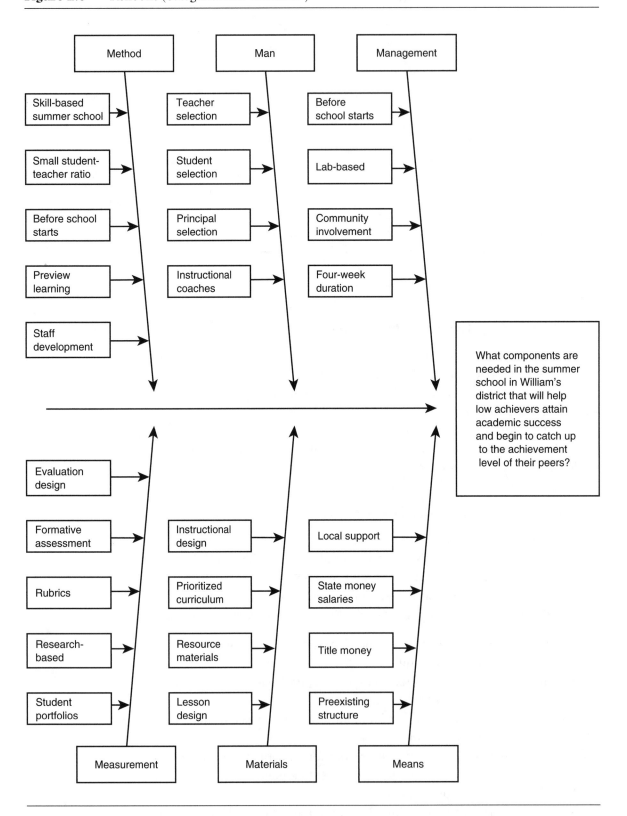

Figure 2.6   Preview Learning and Remediation: A Comparison

Preview Learning	Remediation
• Is connected to grade-level instruction	• Is disconnected from "mainstream" instruction
• Creates a framework for future learning	• Attempts to "fill the gaps" of missed prior learning
• Motivates students to engage in whole-class instruction	• Separates students from regular class instruction
• Is guided by formative assessment	• Is driven by long-term goals
• Is fast-paced with explicit instruction	• Is slow-paced with systematic instruction
• Is designed to accelerate learning	• Tends to increase the learning gap

The PLP will differ from a remedial approach. The basic differences in preview learning and remediation are shown in Figure 2.6.

Exercise Three: Logic Model

"Vision isn't enough—it must be combined with venture. It is not enough to stare up the steps. We must step up the stairs." Vance Havner's wise words help us understand that to move from desire to action, the first steps should be planned and then we should get going. Since design work is erratic and quirky, our model for preview learning in a summer session will be developed to help articulate the goals and lay out the major components identified in the Fishbone Model, to see how they fit together, and determine if the plan will lead to achieving the results the district desires for students in the achievement gap.

Many models exist to assist educators in planning. One of the best models to use, in my opinion, is a Logic Model. Two resources give the planner a thoughtful and well-organized approach to developing a Logic Model. Killion (2002) and the W. K. Kellogg Foundation (www.wkkf.org) are both excellent sources of information. The instructional task force (ITF) in William's district used both models to guide their thinking and frame the district's model. The district's model resembles a basic Logic Model except for two major differences:

1. The model developed by the ITF includes elements of a blueprint.

2. The assumptions in the model used by the ITF about underachievers and higher-order learning are placed at the end of the model. In a basic Logic Model development process, the assumptions are best stated up front.

The planning model for the summer intervention, developed by the ITF, answers many of the previously listed what-if questions. The model (see Figure 2.7) on page 22 includes:

- A research-based summary of the main need to be addressed
- An identification of the desired results

Figure 2.7   Planning Model for William's District

Element	Description
Problem: Statement of Need	• 2,935 students in 51 schools, grades 2–5, in the first quartile of achievement in reading as determined by standardized tests • 46% of the 2,935 students are found in ten inner-city schools • 130,000 students in 228 schools in the U.S., with same type population, have students meeting high academic standards (Reeves, 2004)
Desired Results	• Increase student performance in the fall • Have teachers use new knowledge in regular classrooms • Give a boost to the urban community • Create a network of learners
Review of Literature	Reeves, Marzano, Erickson, Hyerle, Hirsh, English, Thompson, Greggory, Schmoker, Guskey, Dunn, Stiggins, McTighe, Chapman, Killion, Wolfe, Sousa
Planning and Implementation Strategies	Identifying data-based needs; Questioning; Rubrics; Essential questions; Essential learnings; Acquisition lessons; Time of year; Program delivery; Student identification; Teacher selection; Principal selection; Feedback coaches; Lab-based staff development; Evaluation design; Formative assessment; Learning-focused curriculum; Community involvement
Assumptions on Which to Base Innovation	• Low achievers *can* have a high rate of success with learning new skills and content • ALL regular students can master a subject when given sufficient time and appropriate instruction • Learning is increased when teaching is presented in a manner that assists students in organizing, storing, and retrieving knowledge • Time is an important instructional variable • Teachers and students should have high-quality learning opportunities every day • Staff development should play a role in sustained instructional improvement
School and Community Resources	Disaggregated data on low-performing students; Preexisting structure in place for summer school; Title II and V money for materials, supplies, and stipends; Experienced curriculum writers in the system; Qualified program development personnel; Abundant and appropriate materials in a system resource bank; State salary money for personnel; Upper echelon support for productive change; Cooperation with community agencies; Effective staff development program

- A review of the literature and how to apply it to the research on best practices to support a plausible solution for the area of need
- A list of planning and implementation segments
- An identification of district and community resources
- Assumptions about achievers and higher-order learning

Succinctly stated, the model brings together planning, evaluation, and action for the innovation. When the comprehensive document is completed, it will be one of the key methods for the district to use in tracking the progress of the program.

Now that the model has been developed and its conceptual framework designed, plans can be made to enable the ITF to make smart choices and increase the possibility that the students will learn at the desired levels of achievement. It is important to note, however, that the Preview Learning Model will most likely be changed and perfected throughout the process of developing, implementing, evaluating, and refining the innovation. As programming moves forward and the team learns more about the PLP and how it is working, and as different elements of the model are tested for effectiveness, they will discover what every programmer learns sooner or later: some components work as initially conceptualized and some do not! Assumptions may even be determined to be incorrect. With ongoing assessment and paying copious attention to any changes in quantitative data, however, the intervention will become a program that will bring improved learning for the low achiever and be a powerful force for change in William's district and other systems that choose to use it.

MAKING IT "LIVE" FOR YOU:
A PLANNING TEMPLATE

1. Stimulate your own creative thinking by conducting activities that use vertical and horizontal thinking. Use it both independently and with a planning group. Share out ideas created by the group and spend time discussing the thinking. Chart the ideas for future reference.
   - Wisdom Storm (vertical thinking) is on Worksheet 2.1. See page 180 in the Resources.
   - Synectics (horizontal thinking) is on Worksheet 2.2. See page 181 in the Resources.
   - Storytelling (horizontal thinking) assistance is on Worksheet 2.3. See page 182 in the Resources.

2. Develop your own set of Powerful Questions. Pose your questions in the what-if format. A planning template, divided into planning domains, is provided in Worksheet 2.4 (pages 183–187 in the Resources) for your brainstorming session. Use the questions that you and your team generate to examine each domain in depth and to help you simplify the complexity of your work.

3. Complete the following sentence stems:

- The program that we are already operating in our system that, if reformatted, will let us effectively address our problem is _____

  _____

  _____.

- The what-if questions that we generated will lead us to investigate a program that includes the attributes of _____

  _____

  _____.

- An evolutionary program that we currently implement that has the potential to be revolutionary is _____

  _____

  _____.

- The intervention that we already have in place in our district that can accommodate large numbers of students is _____

  _____

  _____.

4. Develop your Fishbone Model.

- Define your problem and put it in the head of the Fishbone in Worksheet 2.5 (see page 188 in the Resources). Analyze the "M" components that you consider to be workable for your system, using the remainder of the figure. You may use Figures 2.3 through 2.5, shown earlier in the chapter, as references.

5. Develop a definition for your intervention.

- Based on the work that you have just completed, define your intervention and list several concepts that are horizontal in nature and that will make it revolutionary. The list from William's district may serve as a guide, if needed.

6. Design the planning model that you will use.

- Killion (2002) provides information that you may want to use to develop a basic Logic Model. The framework for the modified Logic Model used in William's district for planning is provided in Worksheet 2.6 (see page 189 in the Resources) for you to use. This model will assist you in answering your what-if questions and bringing meaning to your Fishbone design. If any design pieces are missing in your planning, this model will make you aware of the lapse so that you can fill the void before you move any further in your work.

Selecting Educators

The Quest for Excellence

Success, real success, in any endeavor
demands more from an individual
than most people are willing to offer—
not more than they are capable of offering.

—James Roche

A RESULTS-BASED SELECTION PROCESS

In a Preview Learning Program (PLP) one essential question that must be asked is, "What procedure can be used to hire the most competent and qualified teachers to teach in a revolutionized summer school?" In William's system, it is understood that the knowledge exists to teach pertinent academic skills to all but a small number of severely disabled children. The research gives good guidance, but it isn't keeping students out of the lowest quartile of achievement in reading or other subjects. William's district is not alone in this category.

Reading is the fundamental skill upon which all formal education depends, and 95 percent of all children should be reading at a level constrained only by their reasoning and listening comprehension abilities (Fletcher & Lyon, 1998). Students in high-risk populations should not be failing at the rate they do

(Nicholson, 1997). There is a key to learning to read for these students. The key involves well-prepared teachers teaching appropriate curriculum, using effective instructional strategies, and giving extra time to students to master the skills. According to Nicholson, this will help the low-achieving group to read as well as their peers who have more advantages. Placing the most effective educators in positions of leadership is within the purview of the administration and policy makers in every system. When the placement occurs, it then puts the onus on program planners and designers in curriculum, instruction, and staff development to produce a workable action plan that will bring about improved learning in the at-risk population. This book describes a lab-based intervention program that incorporates such a plan and offers a strategy for enlisting and selecting educators who have the capacity to bring meaning to lessons in an active, direct, and systematic way.

A STUDENT-FOCUSED OUTCOME

Any outcome must be student-focused—even when the topic is enlisting teachers and selecting personnel. A question will help us develop the correct focus. In this case, the question is directly related to the Preview Learning Program.

The question, "What do we want to see students doing and hear them saying when they have completed the Preview Learning Program?" is important in identifying the qualifications of a teacher who can most effectively facilitate improved learning and student achievement in reading. The key word here is *effective.*

Effectiveness in teaching should not be confused with "highly qualified." There is a difference. A teacher can have proper training and years of experience and still have a high percentage of her students fail to learn. Highly qualified teachers are not always effective. If the teacher is effective, she will have the opportunity to say to one and all, "My students are learning concepts, facts, and skills to a prescribed level—even the economically disadvantaged students." An effective teacher will teach a defined body of knowledge and skills that is based on the best research in the field and use a standard level of achievement as the minimal expectation. Presenting information to students in an order in which they can learn it (Moats, 1999) and being reflective in their own practice are important aspects of teacher effectiveness, as is being involved in continuous professional growth and scholarship designed to improve student learning. James Stronge (2002) writes that effective teachers recognize complexity, communicate clearly, and serve conscientiously. Reeves (2004a) declares that effective teachers are committed to replicating vigorous practices and have a repertoire of strategies keyed to the different ways that content can be difficult. Briefly, it may be said that an effective teacher will enhance student achievement. That is the outcome that should drive the selection process for personnel!

ARTICULATING THE SELECTION PROCESS: WHY IT IS IMPORTANT

There is a fundamental premise about educators and school leaders: *They want to be effective in their profession!* If this is true, why is a selection process needed? With educators wanting to be effective in their profession, why is it not okay to issue a general call for applicants to teach in a specialized program, and then hire the ones with the best credentials and the most experience? There are several reasons why.

1. There are standards for effective teaching that go before us as a banner to guide all who are interested in strengthening the skills of America's teachers. The National Board for Professional Teaching Standards says that teaching is *"Often portrayed as an activity that conserves valued knowledge and skills by transmitting them to succeeding generations. But, it is that and more."* It is the *more* that leads me to suggest that a selection process is important. The potential for greatness in teaching may be tied up in the selection process.

2. One of the cardinal principles of leadership is that it is faster to build on strengths than to compensate for weaknesses. In an intervention program, especially one that focuses on low-achieving and economically deprived youngsters, there is not a minute to waste. The best teachers must be in place and be ready to proceed with the task of effectively teaching these students. There is no time to remediate for teachers. There is only time to work from the growth edge that the teacher has already attained.

3. Each person has natural "talents" (strongest synaptic connections) that can be translated into bona fide strengths. The talents are the most important raw material for strength building. Some teachers have talents in areas that are more aligned with the needs found in an intervention program.

4. Effective teachers are consciously competent (Buckingham & Clifton, 2001). They know what to do to consistently achieve nearly perfect performance, and they can replicate moments of success time and time again. When teachers are consciously competent, they have more opportunities with students to make learning more probable and forgetting less likely.

5. By changing the way we select and channel the careers of teachers through an intervention program, we establish a model for what works that can be adopted or adapted for the entire district.

6. The process is results-driven. Two critical questions form the backbone of this process: *"What is the right thing to do?"* and *"What results do I want?"* Dennis Sparks, Executive Director of the National Staff

Development Council, in *Leading for Results* (2004), gives seven beliefs and abilities that he calls "results skills." Two of them are appropriate here: *clarity of thought regarding intentions and assumptions* and *continuous innovation in the methods used to achieve goals.* The thought behind the selection process is clear. The desired results are clearly stated. The selection process will be innovative, use horizontal thinking, and have results that will raise the achievement level of the at-risk student. Each of these will warrant a continuation of the process.

Richard Elmore (2003) writes that we should "pay attention to who knows what and how that knowledge can strengthen the organization." We must identify these people in our classrooms and administrative positions and use them to influence change in the quality of instruction from teacher to student and teacher to teacher. Marzano, Pickering, and Pollock (2001) write that highly effective teachers can have a profound influence on student learning. Good and Brophy (1986) state: "The myth that teachers do not make a difference in student learning has been refuted" (p. 370). Therefore, the teachers who make a difference in student learning shall be identified and enlisted to work in critical areas, including the intervention program presented in this book. The children in the achievement gap can wait no longer to break the cycle of failure. All educators have a moral obligation to help.

WHAT TEACHERS SHOULD KNOW AND BE ABLE TO DO

As we have seen, effective teachers do things differently, but what is it that they do and what do they know that makes them unique? Marzano, Pickering, and Pollock (2001) and Squires (2005) guide our thinking in what we must see *students* doing and hear them saying. All the works of Doug Reeves and Rick Stiggins have broadened our understanding of assessment, and, likewise, Tom Guskey leads us in looking at quality staff development that affects student achievement. Taken together, their information gives us the knowledge and behaviors we can expect to see in *teachers* that enhance learning for students.

In June 1999, Louisa C. Moats prepared a paper for the American Federation of Teachers titled, "Teaching Reading *Is* Rocket Science: What Expert Teachers of Reading Should Know and Be Able to Do." Earlier, in 1989, the National Board for Professional Teaching Standards issued its policy statement, *What Teachers Should Know and Be Able to Do,* which served as the basis for all the standards development work the organization conducted. There are other studies that may be cited, but the following synthesis of the information from both studies, along with the information from the authors cited above, can illuminate our thinking. Teachers, therefore, should

- Have an understanding of how students develop and learn
- Know the subject they teach and how to teach those subjects to students
- Know how to manage and monitor student learning

Figure 3.1   What Teachers Should Know and Be Able to Do—Preview Learning Program

Have an understanding of how students develop and learn	Know how to regularly assess student progress to enhance student learning
Know the subjects they teach and how to teach those subjects to students	Know how to systematically think about their practice and learn from experience
Know how to manage and monitor student learning	Seek advice of others and draw on educational research and scholarship to improve their practice
Know how to orchestrate learning in group settings	Contribute to school effectiveness by collaborating with parents and other professionals
Know to place a premium on student engagement	Take advantage of community resources

- Know how to orchestrate learning in group settings
- Know to place a premium on student engagement
- Know how to regularly assess student progress to enhance student learning
- Know how to systematically think about their practice and learn from experience
- Seek advice of others and draw on educational research and scholarship to improve their practice
- Contribute to school effectiveness by collaborating with parents and other professionals
- Take advantage of community resources

ASSESSMENT TOOLS TO ENSURE QUALITY IN THE SELECTION PROCESS

A tool must be used that will

- Give meaning to the person, or committee, who will ultimately make the selection
- Be stimulating and thought-provoking for the applicant
- Be a guide for teachers to use to focus on student learning

The development of that tool includes seven steps. The steps may be adapted for any educational program, but the ones listed here are specific to the needs of the Preview Learning Program.

1. Develop a scoring guide for selecting effective teachers. Include six levels, beginning with Level Zero, where teachers give no details or answers to questions, and continue in the guide along a continuum to Level Five, where answers are at the highest level of response. An example of the Personnel Scoring Guide used in William's district is shown in Figure 3.2 on the next page.

Figure 3.2   Personnel Scoring Guide—Preview Learning Program

Level Five	The teacher uses precise language to describe four or more strategies that are indicative of cutting-edge research and that show outside-the-box thinking.
Level Four	The teacher uses precise language to describe four or more strategies that are indicative of cutting-edge research.
Level Three	The teacher talks about three ideas that show creative and motivational strategies.
Level Two	The teacher talks about two details, but the details may be sketchy and/or nondefinitive.
Level One	The teacher talks about one detail, but the talk may be confused, or even wrong, and lack coherence.
Level Zero	The teacher gives no detail or answer.

2. Review the 10 bulleted summary statements on pages 28–29 that detail what teachers should know and be able to do. Develop a chart for each item that includes the identifying statement, a sentence stem using the identifying statement that will give the applicant a cue for thinking, and a clue for an applicant to begin thinking, and answers in column three that you may use to review the teacher's responses. This will be the Preview Learning Program Scoring Guide. Figures 3.3 through 3.10 give you eight examples of completed guides.

Figure 3.3   Preview Learning Program Scoring Guide (Understanding student learning)

What Teachers Should Know and Do	Sentence Stem	Possible Answers
Have an understanding of how students develop and learn	Students learn best when they . . .	• Set their own academic goals
		• Develop strategies to meet goals
		• Reflect on their academic performance
		• Are taught according to their preferred learning style
		• Are not intimidated
		• Are taught at the correct level of difficulty
		• Know what it is that they are supposed to learn
		• Self-regulate

Figure 3.4   Preview Learning Program Scoring Guide (Managing and monitoring learning)

What Teachers Should Know and Do	Sentence Stem	Possible Answers
How to manage and monitor student learning	Teachers can best manage and monitor student learning by . . .	• Conducting periodic reviews with students to confirm their grasp of the material and to identify gaps in knowledge and understanding
		• Reviewing student performance data and using the data to make needed adjustments in instruction
		• Keeping track of student learning for the purposes of feedback to students on their individual progress
		• Questioning students during classroom discussions to check for understanding of material taught
		• Circulating around classroom during seatwork and engaging in one-to-one contact with students about work
		• Assigning, collecting, and correcting homework, recording completion and grade

Figure 3.5   Preview Learning Program Scoring Guide (Orchestrating learning in groups)

What Teachers Should Know and Do	Sentence Stem	Possible Answers
How to orchestrate learning in group settings	The best way for teachers to orchestrate learning for students in group settings is to . . .	• Involve all students in a structured manner in presentations, discussions, and recitations
		• Provide both oral and written directions when feasible
		• Break directions into student-manageable chunks and provide visual clues
		• Give assignments in two parts: a basic one for all students and a second one that can be completed for extra credit
		• Establish rules, procedures, and consequences for the classroom and school

Figure 3.6   Preview Learning Program Scoring Guide (Using student engagement)

What Teachers Should Know and Do	Sentence Stem	Possible Answers
Know to place a premium on student engagement	Teachers effectively engage students when they . . .	• Use essential questions that are drawn from topics and general levels of knowledge
		• Encourage students to question and reflect on what they are learning or constructing
		• Use specialized project-based learning
		• Have students become actively involved in assessing their own learning
		• Help students see patterns, connections, and transferability of knowledge
		• Draw on multiple modalities
		• Allow students to question what they are doing
		• Center facts and activities around a specific topic of study
		• Involve them in authentic tasks

Figure 3.7 Preview Learning Program Scoring Guide (Assessing student progress)

What Teachers Should Know and Do	Sentence Stem	Possible Answers
How to regularly assess student progress to enhance student learning	Strategies to authentically assess student learning include . . .	• Exhibits
		• Performances and demonstrations
		• Journals and logs
		• Projects and portfolios
		• Problem-solving processes
		• Graphic organizers
		• Involving students in designing rubrics with criteria and indicators of success
		• Involving students in a self-directed study based on a rubric of excellence that they constructed

Figure 3.8   Preview Learning Program Scoring Guide (Reflecting on practice)

What Teachers Should Know and Do	Sentence Stem	Possible Answers
How to systematically think about their practice and learn from experience	**Reflective practice requires . . .**	• Deliberate pauses
		• Open perspective or open-mindedness
		• Thinking processes of inquiry, metacognition, analysis, integration, and synthesis
		• Self-observation and analysis of one's behavior along with the perceived consequences
		• Awareness of one's decision-making process for determining differentiated instructional objectives and strategies
		• New insights and understandings and higher-level thinking processes
		• Actions that improve students' learning

Figure 3.9 Preview Learning Program Scoring Guide (Using research and scholarship)

What Teachers Should Know and Do	Sentence Stem	Possible Answers
Seek advice of others and draw on educational research and scholarship to improve their practice	**The teacher who keeps abreast of current research-based practices about teaching and learning will . . .**	• Be better able to plan for instruction
		• Be able to explain why they decide to use a certain strategy and teach in a particular way
		• Better understand potential problems and possible solutions to problems
		• Collaborate more freely and be less likely to practice teaching in isolation
		• Realize that data are essential to school improvement

Figure 3.10 Preview Learning Program Scoring Guide (Collaborating)

What Teachers Should Know and Do	Sentence Stem	Possible Answers
Contribute to school effectiveness by collaborating with parents and other professionals	**Examples of artifacts that can be used to elicit conversations about school effectiveness include . . .**	• Instructional units
		• Teacher-made tests
		• Letters to parents
		• Pictures of classroom and students
		• Cassette tapes or videotapes of tutoring sessions
		• Videos of student performances
		• Lists of class rules and consequences
		• Portfolios
		• Strategic plans

3. Develop a response page that will be sent to all teachers and administrative applicants. This will be a reflection piece for the applicants and includes the sentence stems that you developed for column two in step two above. A sample response page, "Reflecting on Our Profession," is shown for your reference in Figure 3.11. In preparing the response sheet, remember to give ample room for the respondents to thoughtfully complete the sentences. You may also direct them to use a separate sheet if more response space is needed.

Figure 3.11 Reflecting on Our Profession

Control Number ___

REFLECTING ON OUR PROFESSION

This year's summer school will be a preview learning program, which will prepare youngsters for the beginning of the next school year. To assist in making meaningful placements of teachers, please complete the following sentence stems. It is important that you give thoughtful, research-based responses. You may collaborate with your colleagues or review research to give your best responses. The answers, however, should be your own. Please type your work.

Name _____ School_____

≺   Students learn best when they . . .

≺   Teachers can best manage and monitor student learning by . . .

≺   The best way for teachers to orchestrate learning for students in group settings is . . .

≺ Teachers effectively engage students when they . . .

≺ Strategies to authentically assess student learning include . . .

≺ Reflective practice requires . . .

≺ The teacher who keeps abreast of current research-based practices about teaching and learning will . . .

≺ Examples of artifacts that can be used to elicit conversations about school effectiveness include . . .

Thank you for your thoughtful responses. Please return your reflection to the summer school office at the Teacher Center by Monday, March 18, at 4 p.m. You may fax your responses to (fax number), or e-mail them to (e-mail address).

If you expect the answers to be typed, that should be noted in the directions. A letter to the applicants (Figure 3.12) must be included with the response page, giving specific directions on completing the page. It is important to note that one of the purposes of completing the response form is to expand professional knowledge; therefore, it will be appropriate for the applicants to do some research, if necessary, to complete the sentence stems.

Figure 3.12   Educator Memo

To: Certified Personnel

From: Marti Richardson

Re: Employment Process

You have an opportunity to apply to teach in the new laboratory-based learning program that will focus on preview learning for youngsters. As indicated in the recent informational meetings, the dates for the Preview Learning Program are July 8–August 2. Two prerequisite staff development days will be held in the spring after school is out—sometime during the week of May 27–31. There will be a stipend paid for those two days.

Staff development will also be a part of the contract day for the four weeks of the summer program. Afternoon labs will offer specific training designed to assist you to better meet the needs of the students who will be served in the program.

Enclosed you will find a set of open-ended responses, which you must complete and return to the summer school office at the teacher center. Please note the directions on the reflection form. Your responses to the questions will be scored according to a rubric; therefore, you will want to present your best thinking on the form. The quality of your answers will be used as a data source in the hiring process. *Please type your responses.*

A committee will review all relevant data following the submission deadline and begin notifying applicants of their employment status by early April.

For your information, there will be (enter number) sites: (list sites here)

Please send your completed reflection forms to: (address)

The deadline for receiving the reflection forms is Monday, March 18, at 4 p.m. You may fax your responses to (fax number), or e-mail them to (e-mail address).

Good luck as you prepare your responses.

4. Prepare to advertise the employment process.
    a. Identify the number of students who qualify for the PLP.
    b. Determine the number of sites that will be necessary to accommodate students in order to keep the student-teacher ratio to a maximum of 8:1.
    c. Select sites. Sites should be convenient for the economically disadvantaged students, since transportation may be a challenge for them.
    d. Inform current principals throughout the system about the program and give them a list of students in their building who qualify to be involved in the PLP.
    e. Prepare the announcement for the selection process for employing teachers. Give complete information.

5. Identify a management committee of facilitators (no more than four people) to work collaboratively to score the response pages. It is important to remove the names of the applicants from their response sheets before scoring occurs, to ensure objectivity and privacy. A control number on each response sheet and a master list of matching names and control numbers will expedite this step.

6. Score the response pages by using the Preview Learning Scoring Guide. Be aware that in column three of the Scoring Guide there may be appropriate closing statements for the sentence stems that you did not include in your responses. As you examine the applicants' responses, allow such answers to be counted correct if, in your educated opinion, they are correct. List the total score in the upper right-hand corner of each response page. Identify the author of the work only after the scoring has been completed.

7. Rank-order the collection of response pages by putting the highest scores first.

8. Transfer the rank-ordered information to the Preview Learning Summary Scoring Sheet (Figure 3.13). Record the control number from the reflection sheet (Figure 3.11). Write the individual's name and list the scores for each response to the right of the name. The total score should be used to determine the rank order.

In William's district, the applicants with the highest summary scores, if they were appropriately certified, were invited to be feedback coaches or site administrators.

MAKING IT "LIVE" FOR YOU: A PLANNING TEMPLATE

1. List the things that you are currently doing in your district in the selection process to identify effective educators who will work in specific areas of need.

Figure 3.13 Preview Learning Summary Scoring Sheet

Control Number and Name	Scores for Individual Questions as Determined by the Scoring Rubric								
	1	2	3	4	5	6	7	8	Total

2. Review Figure 3.1, "What Teachers Should Know and Be Able to Do." Add any research-based statements that will support your process of selecting effective personnel. Use the newly developed chart in your planning.

3. Review Figure 3.2, "Personnel Scoring Guide." Make adjustments to meet the needs of your district's intervention program. Use your enhanced document in your planning.

4. Develop a form to use with your selection process. Figure 3.11 may be used as an example.

5. Develop your memo to teachers announcing the opportunity to be involved in an intervention program for low achievers. Figure 3.12 may be used as a guide.

6. Use Figure 3.13, "Preview Learning Summary Scoring Sheet," as a guide to develop a summary scoring sheet that is specific to the needs of your district.

Developing a Purpose-Driven Curriculum

*There are no such things as limits to growth
because there are no limits on the human capacity
for intelligence, imagination, and wonder.*

—Former President Ronald Reagan

ACQUIRING KNOWLEDGE

We are all familiar with Albert Einstein's oft-quoted definition of insanity—doing the same thing over and over again and expecting different results. There is no place where this statement is truer than in the ways we work with our low-achieving students. As a profession, we are woefully inept at helping students in the achievement gap experience in-depth learning of skills that will orient them to higher-order problem solving and decision making. We spend very little time engaging them in activities that connect them to the knowledge that validates the experiences they bring to learning, yet we know that their direct involvement is important to their continued growth and development. The reasons for our deficits are not the topic for our discussion here. Finding ways to engage these students in strategies that help them acquire, produce, use, and communicate knowledge is, however, of the utmost importance.

The curriculum must be presented to students in the achievement gap in a different way! They need a curriculum that changes the *when, how,* and *what* they are taught. The students should be taught more, not less (Thompson, 2005). They must be introduced to what they are going to learn in an intentional way and then deliberately taught what they will learn. By accelerating the curriculum and introducing strategically selected essential skills and concepts before the skills and concepts are taught for mastery, the teaching can be direct and explicit. Boyles (2005) calls this concept *scaffolding.* This is a new way of thinking for many educators, and would be a revolutionary approach for most districts. Scaffolding may entail writing a new curriculum that is specific for the at-risk student. In William's district, it did.

The Preview Learning Program (PLP) selected to be the intervention strategy has all the elements of an advance learning program and includes scaffolded learning for students through a structured and focused curriculum, designated instructional strategies, and formative assessment for teachers to use daily. It is a preview learning program in reading, with skills and concepts presented in a new way to the targeted youngsters. With proper monitoring of the students' active learning, success is ensured for each child who is involved.

PLANNING THE CURRICULUM

The curriculum must be planned and developed to meet the academic needs of the poor and minority students who typically characterize the population of students caught in the achievement gap. Other children may also benefit. The skills and concepts that are routinely taught to the students who have been "left behind" should be *rethought, reframed, and realigned* to achieve the desired results. The careful review of the curriculum will be a unique process, and the most efficient way to approach the review is by asking questions. General questioning, however, will not be sufficient because curriculum planning is highly complex and uses both divergent and convergent thinking as ideas are generated, expanded on, and then refined for adaptation into instructional patterns.

In William's district, the innovation task force (ITF) asked questions that required more and more answers as the group got deeper into the process. Each question stimulated discussion and became the basis for yet another question. The teachers' in-depth analysis of a quality curriculum for their PLP helped them refine the planning process and gave them an effective and strategic way to organize their thinking to simplify an intricate task. The list of simple, yet profound and powerful questions that were generated by the ITF to use as a guide to their planning is found in Figure 4.1 (a–e).

ORGANIZING AND CATEGORIZING THE QUESTIONS

A list of planning questions (Solomon, 2003) will reveal different components of the curriculum that must be systematically analyzed during the planning stage. The analysis helps to

Figure 4.1a   Powerful Questions to Guide Thinking in Developing a Curriculum for Preview Learning

Domain	Powerful Question
Standards	Do new standards require new curricula?
	What are our state standards for reading?
	Will the new standards require more time with the curriculum from some students than others?
	Do new standards require new ways of assessing student learning and then using results to change instruction when students are not "getting it"?
	Do new standards require teachers to work inter/intra grade levels? If so, what kind of coordination will be required and how will it occur?
Curriculum	Do we need an intervention curriculum framework or will the framework used by the district suffice?
	From where will the new curricula for the preview learning come?
	What assumptions are we already making about the curriculum?
	Do students need to be grouped in new ways to provide them access to the new curricula?
	Since the nation cannot raise achievement across the board without paying attention to the significant percentage of students enrolled in urban schools, are there areas of the curriculum that are more specific to the needs of this population of students?
	Should there be different forms of curricula (electronic, hardbound, etc.)?
	Will our curriculum delivery design include more than one site?
	Will we teach less content? More content?
	Will we use informational texts as an integral part of the curriculum?
	Will we pose essential questions?

- Investigate the desirability of developing your own focus-driven intervention curriculum
- Focus the group's efforts
- Bypass ineffective, obsolete, or superfluous steps
- Determine whether the curriculum design will be evolutionary or revolutionary (see Chapter 2 for a review of the definition of these terms)

All the questions can be organized through the use of a "question wheel." This wheel will allow a task force to work economically and personalize the program to the district's needs. Several mindsets may be explored and answers can be spread out categorically. The wheel is a precursor to an action plan.

Figure 4.1b   Powerful Questions to Guide Thinking in Developing a Curriculum for Preview Learning

Domain	Powerful Question
Instruction	What grouping patterns are likely to work?
	How will time be used differently for a differentiated group of students?
	Should we develop another statement of subject-specific principles and beliefs that guide instruction, or will the statement in the district's master plan support our work?
	How will our strategy support the master teaching that occurs during the regular school year?
	What are the implications of different uses of time for the way teachers' work is organized?
	Will we instruct with technology?
	Will we teach the same thing at the same time every day?
	Will the instruction be theme-based?
	Will we differentiate reading instruction?
	Will we include strategies to support multiple intelligences? Learning styles?
	Will we plan lessons to include performance tasks?
	Do we know which instructional strategies will increase student achievement?
	How can we teach through multiple modalities what will actively engage the neural pathways of each child?

Figure 4.1c shows a question wheel that was partially developed by William's district, using the questions that were taken from Figure 4.1a and 4.1b and placing them categorically in order on the wheel. When all the questions have been categorized and written on the wheel, a group can easily determine if more questions are still required for further analysis in a specific category. All thinking should be focused on possible actions and outcomes for the district.

DEVELOPING A QUESTION WHEEL

To develop a question wheel, list the overarching question in the center of the wheel. The ITF in William's district chose the question, which would drive all the questions on the wheel: *"What questions can we ask that will help us design an*

Figure 4.1c   The Question Wheel

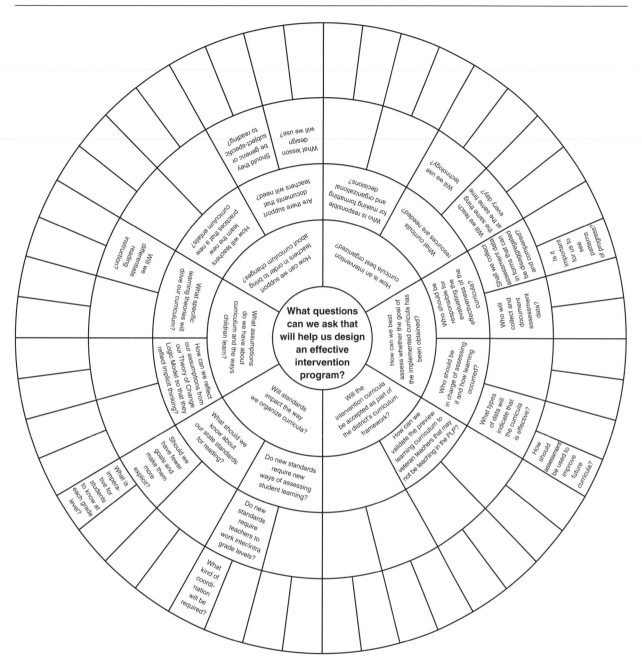

effective intervention program?" The *first order* of questions is placed on the circle immediately surrounding the main question. These are the questions that define a category to be explored more in orders two, three, and four.

To determine the questions for each of the second through fourth orders, rephrase the question that has just been written and re-ask it covertly with an *if,* or similar word. For example, if the question is, *"Will standards impact the way we organize curricula?"* we would insert an *if* and say *"If standards impact the way we organize curricula . . ."* and use that question as a springboard for developing

Figure 4.1d   Powerful Questions to Guide Thinking in Developing a Curriculum for Preview Learning

Domain	Powerful Question
Professional Development	What do we need to provide teachers so they can structure their teaching, learning, and assessing to obtain outcomes and principles identified in the standards and framework?
	Are there support documents that teachers will need? Should they be generic or subject-specific to reading?
	How will the teachers learn the new skills and practices the program entails?
	Will we have learning teams?
	What resources are available to tell us the criteria for effective professional development?
Assessment	How will we assess the quality of instruction?
	From where will the assessment strategies come?
	Should we collect assessment data in forms that can be disaggregated and compared so that we can develop patterns of student progress as students participate in curriculum activities?
	How will we keep progress records on what the child achieves during the Preview Learning Program?
	How can we best assess whether the goal of the implemented curricula has been attained?
	Will alternate assessment be used?
	Who should be in charge of assessing if and how learning occurred?
	How should assessment and evaluation data be used to improve the curricula?

the question to follow, which may be, *"What should we know about state standards for reading?"* Figure 4.2 shows the thought process.

The process is the same each time a question is asked and written on the next order of the wheel. There are two places provided on the wheel for new questions that further analyze the question of the previous order. Not all spaces have to be filled in, however. When an examination of a question has been completed, simply stop asking questions.

For clarity in planning, a chart (Figure 4.3) is included to illustrate another way of developing a structure for asking questions in design work. The same thought process illustrated in Figure 4.2 is applicable in charting the questions.

Figure 4.1e Powerful Questions to Guide Thinking in Developing a Curriculum for Preview Learning

Domain	Powerful Question
Evaluation	What student learning outcomes in knowledge and skills can we expect in a Preview Learning Program? Should these outcomes be expressed as general outcomes or specific outcomes?
	How can we show the breadth and depth contained in the desired learning outcomes?
	How will we ensure the quality of the instructional strategies that are designed into the delivery system of the curriculum?
	What lesson design will we use? How will we know it is effective?
	Should we have fewer goals for ourselves and make them more explicit?
	What types of evidence will indicate that the curriculum we have developed is effective?
	Who should be responsible for evaluating the effectiveness of the curricula and for collecting and documenting assessment data?
	How should evaluation data be used to improve the curricula?
	How will we know if the curriculum is effective?
Other	When problems arise during our planning and developmental period, how will we address them?
	What resources are available?
	Are grant funds available for curriculum development?
	What are the planning deadlines for this group?
	How can we validate the preview learning curriculum to veteran teachers that may not be teaching in the preview program?
	How can we reflect our assumptions from our Theory of Change Logic Model so that they reflect implicit thinking?

Figure 4.2 Questioning Thought Process

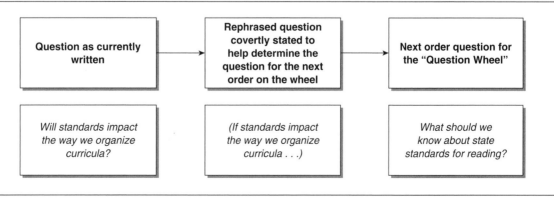

Figure 4.3a   Preview Learning: The Question Wheel in Chart Form

Overarching Question: What questions can we ask that will help us design an effective intervention program?

First Order Question	Second Order Question	Third Order Question	Fourth Order Question
Will standards impact the way we organize curricula?	What should we know about our state standards for reading?	Should we have fewer goals and make them more explicit?	What is imperative for students to know at each grade level?
	Do new standards require new ways of assessing student learning?	Do new standards require teachers to work inter/intra grade levels?	What kind of coordination will be required?
Will the intervention curricula be accepted as part of the district's curriculum framework?	How can we validate the preview learning curriculum to veteran teachers who may not be teaching in the PLP?		
How can we best assess whether the goal of the implemented curricula has been obtained?	Who should be in charge of assessing if and how learning occurred?	What types of data will indicate that the curricula are effective?	How should assessment be used to improve future curricula?
	Who should be responsible for evaluating the effectiveness of the curricula?	Who will collect and document assessment data?	
		Shall we collect assessment data in forms that can be disaggregated and compared?	Is it important for us to see patterns of progress?
How are intervention curricula best organized?	What curricula resources are needed?	Will we teach the same thing at the same time every day?	
		Will we use technology?	
	Who is responsible for making formatting and organizational decisions?		

Figure 4.3b   Preview Learning: The Question Wheel in Chart Form

Overarching Question: What questions can we ask that will help us design an effective intervention program?

First Order Question	Second Order Question	Third Order Question	Fourth Order Question
How can we support teachers in order to bring about curriculum changes?	Are there support documents that teachers will need?	What lesson design will we use?	
		Should they be generic or subject-specific to reading?	
	How will teachers learn the new practices that a new curriculum entails?		
What assumptions do we have about curriculum and the ways children learn?	What specific learning theories will drive our curriculum?	Will we differentiate reading instruction?	
	How can we reflect our assumptions from our Theory of Change Logic Model so that they reflect implicit thinking?		

CHARACTERISTICS OF A PREVIEW CURRICULUM

Years of research tell us what must be included in an effective curriculum. This research is applicable to a preview curriculum reading program and should:

1. Be a purpose-driven curriculum

2. Be aligned with content-specific, grade-level standards

3. Include effective teaching strategies

4. Have the knowledge and skills that children should learn at each grade level clearly outlined and presented

5. Be written in a format that is consistent from grade to grade

6. Be designed for awareness, not mastery

7. Spring from essential questions

8. Have differentiated strategies that link directly to the brain research on how learning occurs

9. Provide multiple opportunities for assessment

PLANNING ELEMENTS

Let's briefly explore these nine planning elements.

1. An effective preview learning curriculum will be purpose-driven. Squires (2005) tells us that having a purpose for curriculum is important to planning a coherent curriculum. Building learning experiences that will help struggling students achieve academic success will contribute to the purpose. These students bring deficiencies in academic background knowledge that hamper their achievement (Marzano, 2004). Enhancing that background knowledge must be the focus of the curriculum and all components of the PLP. A variety of purposeful experiences to directly add to the knowledge of these youngsters is the least of the requirements for their learning.

The entire development process for this focused curriculum may be viewed through three lenses. Jacobs (1997) mentions two of these:

- A zoom lens into a yearly curriculum for a particular grade. In reading, direct vocabulary instruction, along with scaffolding of learning (Boyles, 2005), will be caught in the zoom lens for enhancing background knowledge.
- A wide-angle lens to see the perspective for grades K–12. The strategies that are used in a PLP must be continuous over many years.

To these two lenses, a macro must be added. A macro lens on a camera is used to produce optimum definition of a subject when it is photographed at a magnification of approximately 1:1. A macro lens dedicated to developing curriculum that will affect *each* low achiever will highlight disaggregated data specific to each child (Audet & Jordan, 2003; Bernhardt, 2003b; and Johnson, 2002), identify skill gaps, and give appropriate ways to close the gap (Boyles, 2005). In other words, this close-up look will provide the information necessary to develop a new program, a parallel curriculum if you please, that will be specific to the needs of this underserved group. The focus of this third lens is critical in revolutionizing the way we work in classrooms and schools across the country.

2. An effective Preview Learning curriculum will be aligned with content-specific, grade-level standards. Standards exist in today's legislation. They are a part of every school system, state, and region. Doug Reeves (2002), an expert in academic standards, gives an objective look at the topic in *The Leader's Guide to Standards: A Blueprint for Educational Equity and Excellence.* One of the striking concepts in his book is that standards can trigger opportunities for success to flourish! A Preview Learning Program is all about success for a group of youngsters who have experienced very little of it in school. If standards will give this group an opportunity to flourish, then standards should be the foundation of all the material presented to them for new learning.

In the design of a new curriculum framework, every student must be *"assured that they will have high-quality opportunities to learn and be assessed in relation to the standards"* (Carr & Harris, 2001). Federal guidelines have ensured the standards, but youngsters who are behind in academic achievement are being assessed just like students who are average and above in knowledge growth. Now, it is okay to assess them that way if they have been afforded "high-quality opportunities to learn" as Carr and Harris put it. Too often, though, underachieving students work on skills and fail to master them. Then they work on the same skills again, with mastery still absent. This puts them in a downward spiral, with no hope of ever catching up. A Preview Learning Program, especially in the area of reading, with an accompanying comprehensive curriculum, can assist students in attaining standards specific to their grade level.

The design committee for the PLP in William's district was guided by Solomon's (2003) work and asked critical questions about standards to help the educators become more strategic in their planning. Some of these questions appear earlier in this chapter. The specific questions on standards have been extrapolated and charted for easy reference in Figure 4.4. They are listed for you to use as a springboard for discussions with your groups as they ponder using standards to make a difference in the lives of students.

3. An effective Preview Learning curriculum will include effective teaching principles. If we are to be successful with academically at-risk students, instructional strategies must be methodically included with the written curriculum, and *all* elements of the plan must reflect what is known about how learning occurs. The ITF in William's district honored this concept. The group selected 10 effective teaching principles (Figure 4.5) to help them in designing productive

Figure 4.4 Standards, the Curricula, and the Preview Learning Program

• Do new standards require new curricula?	• Do new standards require teachers to work inter/intra grade levels?
• From where will the new curricula come?	• What kind of coordination will be required for the above and how will it occur?
• Will the new standards require more time from some students than others?	• Do new standards require new ways of assessing student results to change instruction when the students are not "getting it"?

instructional strategies. A match of the elements of a PLP, along with the purposes of an effective Preview Learning model, let them know that their work was in alignment in all the components. The correlation chart gives credence to the validity of the design used by William's district.

4. An effective Preview Learning curriculum will include knowledge and skills that children should learn at each grade level clearly outlined and prioritized. It is important to articulate what students must know and be able to do when they have successfully completed designated objectives for each subject at every grade level. To do this, a Prioritized Curriculum must be developed, founded on the premise that curriculum, instruction, assessment, and staff development will be linked together to improve student achievement. Max Thompson's and Julia Thomason's (1998) *Learning-Focused Elementary Schools* presents a model of a prioritized curriculum with K–12 benchmarks. Grade- and subject-specific objectives and skills are designated as E (essential), I (important), or C (compact). The E is the top 50 percent of the skills or concepts most essential for the student to master. The I represents the next 30 percent of the skills or concepts that are important. The compact skills or concepts (C) include at least 20 percent of the desired learning. Thompson reminds us that when planning a prioritized curriculum, especially for low achievers, it is important to

- Code curriculum and allocate time accordingly. Using the categories described above, analyze the most important skills and concepts, and rank them. To do this effectively, view the curriculum as a continuum of more than one level. Include the previous grades and the grades following to bring coherence (Beane, 1995) to the process. Once decisions have been made about what is truly critical for the knowledge, label each skill or concept with the E, I, or C. Spend 60 to 70 percent of the time in previewing the E's for the at-risk child (Thompson, 2005).
- Plan for and teach *essentials* first. Essentials are rudimentary skills or concepts considered imperative to knowledge and understanding. In Preview Learning, the essentials should be accelerated. A timely follow-up with focused and research-based strategies will make ultimate

Figure 4.5   Principles of Learning Addressed in a Preview Learning Program

Learning Principle*	Elements Found in PLP	Academic Purpose
– Increased opportunity to learn content is correlated positively with increased student achievement. The more content covered, the greater the potential for student learning.	– Less is more	– To increase the potential for student learning
– Students learn more when they are actively engaged during an instructional task.	– Hands-on activities related to vocabulary development. – Teachers use allocated time differently.	– To increase the potential for student learning.
– Students can become independent learners through instruction that is carefully scaffolded.	– Dialogue between teacher/student and student/teacher	– To accomplish reading goals that are impossible without assistance.
– All students can master a subject given sufficient time and appropriate instruction.	– Careful content match between student's achievement level and task assignment.	– To present content in small steps.
– Students learn more in classes in which teachers directly teach skills.	– Group students according to skills closely related to the curriculum.	– To have effective instruction in low-ability classes (Gamoran, 1992).
– Learning is increased when teaching is presented in a manner that assists students in organizing, storing, and retrieving knowledge.	– Use of essential questions, graphic organizers, advance organizers, organizing words, cues to students, and post organizers (lesson closure).	– To give learners prior knowledge to bring to the task of acquiring new knowledge (Beck, 1986).
– Students can become independent learners through instruction that is explicit.	– Written curriculum presents information in small steps and provides opportunity to practice after each step.	– To assist students in processing information to increase the likelihood that the information will be transferred to long-term memory.
– Teaching sameness both within and across the subjects promotes the students' ability to access relevant knowledge in problem solving situations.	– Skills are pretaught that will be taught for mastery during regular class time.	– To help students differentiate the essential from the non-essential in organizing skills and knowledge.
– Time is an important instructional variable.	– Students are engaged in diversified learning activities 90–95% of class time	– To optimize teacher interactions with students.
– High and moderate success rates are correlated positively with student learning outcomes.	– Students have precise and continuous assessment of academic skills in order to increase the potential for success.	– To prepare students for a successful regular classroom experience.
*Adapted from the work of Ellis et al., which may be found at http://idea.uoregon.edu/~ncite/documents/techren/tech06.html		

mastery of the essentials more probable. The *importants* can be de-emphasized without putting the student in immediate peril. The *compact* skills or concepts are the "nice-to-knows" that add interest to the topic. They are not necessary for mastery, *but* a caution is in order to remind us that the nice-to-knows are often the materials that motivate a child and meet an effective need. The compact information can be infused into the curriculum in other ways.

- Give the learner who is more at risk a greater allocation of time for mastering the E's. During the regular year, teach key vocabulary words two to four days in advance, and use the words in context during the lesson. Use graphic organizers frequently to reinforce the learning. In William's district, the four-week period prior to the start of school provides low-achieving youngsters with an opportunity to preview all the reading skills that will be taught during the first six weeks of school. When students "meet" the skill again during the regular school year, they are immediately motivated to move forward because of their advance hands-on work with the material.

In Chapter 1, we met William and silently "observed" his reading lesson on whales. We may recall that the story for the day was about Willie, a large humpback whale, who was worried because he was losing his body hair. When the teacher presented the story, there was no structure in place to assist her in teaching the story's concepts. Therefore, the skills that were included in the story were overlooked, and vocabulary instruction was not in evidence. The teaching was unfocused throughout the lesson. A prioritized curriculum for the Grade 2 reading program could have made a difference in William's academic gain during the lesson because he already had an interest in the topic. An excerpt from a structured curriculum plan for this lesson, based on the concept of a prioritized curriculum, might look like the information that is found in Figure 4.6. With the E's, I's, and C's identified the teacher can teach explicitly, focus on what is important, and be strategic in pacing the lesson.

5. An effective Preview Learning curriculum will be written in a teacher-friendly format that is consistent from grade to grade. Once the curriculum has been defined and prioritized, lessons should be developed for the essential skills that will be taught in the PLP. Instructional plans will prevent teachers from having to grapple with "How do I teach this skill?" or "What should I do next?" In my opinion, an acquisition lesson design is the best developmental design to use as students acquire new knowledge. It can be used as a learning plan to organize and structure an array of activities that focus on the E's. A plan of this type may allow teachers to do away with a random assortment of well-intended activities that have no purpose or structure otherwise.

Another reason to use a common format for a lesson comes from English (2000), who reminds us that research reveals that teachers are likely to be dependent upon a textbook for the actual day-to-day work plan. English's insight gives rise to my assumption that teachers would not be as textbook-dependent if, among other things, the curriculum were prioritized; daily,

Figure 4.6 Whales—One Lesson of a Prioritized Curriculum—Grade 4

Rank	Vocabulary	Concepts	Skills*
Essential	• whale • mammal • lungs • breathe • sleek	• Whales are mammals. • Whales breathe air. • Whales live in water, but they are not fish • Whales have hair, but not as much as land mammals. • Whales have almost ho hair as adults.	• Long "e" • Silent "e" • Consonant blends "wh," "br," and "sl"
Important	• devour • squeaks • blowholes • dorsal fin • migrate • sparse	• There are different kinds of whales • The humpback whale has a hump as part of its dorsal fin. • Whales are social and playful animals. • Many whales travel long distances each year from cold water to warm water. • Whales "sing."	• Synonyms • Compound words
Compact	• pod • consume • sieve • species • protected • filtered • breaching • spy hopping • lobtailing • streamlined • cetaceans	• Humpback whales are a protected species. • The humpback whale has a heart with four chambers. • Swimming and other water activities are streamlined. • Whales eat only food from the water that is appropriate for them.	• Syllabication when adding "ed" to a word

NOTE: *Skills are cumulative. Each priority level includes the skills of the previous level.

skill-specific lessons were provided; and common lesson formats were supported and strategically used throughout the district. Providing these structural elements makes the curriculum teacher-friendly and gives the teachers added opportunities to work effectively with individual students to develop their unique skills and abilities.

The Instructional Task Force (ITF) in William's district developed daily lessons for their PLP for Grades 2 through 5. A skill-specific sample of a daily lesson plan for Grade 4 may be found in Chapter 5. As you review the lessons, please pay attention to the variety of scaffolding strategies, such as playing to the multiple intelligences and learning styles that are addressed, as well as the relevance of the lessons to the current brain research. The four-week, half-day curriculum design for the PLP includes a day-to-day specific lesson plan for teachers for only a portion of the program.

In the latter part of the PLP, the prepared lessons begin to have gaps in the information that is included in the structured learning plan. For example, whereas the lessons for weeks one and two give strategies for *active participation,* beginning with week three, those strategies are not included in the lesson plan. The gaps increase daily through the final week. On days 18 through 20, the template includes the skills and vocabulary, but the remainder of the template is blank. Teachers plan collaboratively by grade levels on what to include in the blank sections. This scaffolding process provides teachers with an opportunity to begin with adequately defined curriculum content and to gain experience with a "tightened" relationship between the written curriculum, the taught curriculum, and its alignment to assessment (English, 2000), but then affords them the autonomy to use teaching methods of their choosing to achieve a common outcome.

6. An effective Preview Learning curriculum will be designed for awareness, not mastery. A Preview Learning curriculum should be designed to ensure that every child ultimately has the opportunity to master essential skills for his or her grade level. This is done through introducing skills in advance, thus giving them a scaffold on which to build new, more permanent learning. The variety of ways in which the students receive information, coupled with multiple ways for them to articulate their learning (Boyles, 2005), allows them to make connections that will ultimately support their long-term learning.

At the beginning of a Preview Learning segment, teachers often get frustrated because Johnnie or Susie is not mastering the skill. Teachers must be reminded frequently to refocus on the purpose of the program: *to introduce youngsters to new information so that they can successfully create their own scaffold for mastery learning at a later time.* The Acquisition Lesson Design sets up a pattern to help the student attain that success.

7. An effective Preview Learning curriculum will spring from essential questions. If one begins with the assumption that *every* learner can think critically and come to read with understanding—even the low achiever—then the next logical step in designing a curriculum is to ask an important question about what is needed. Not just any question will do. It must be a global question that springs from the upper levels of Bloom's (1954) Taxonomy and set the stage for asking further questions that provide facts that will ultimately answer the larger question. It must be an *essential question!* In planning the PLP, the task force asked the essential question: *"What curriculum will increase the capacity of a low-achieving student to read fluently with great understanding?"* This question was a powerful tool for them because it was a well-constructed question, it focused on the essence of the task, and it opened the door for several smaller questions (foundation questions). These foundation questions gave the curriculum-writing committee their direction for decision making.

A visual of the relationship between one essential question and the foundation questions is shown in a cluster map in Figure 4.7. The essential question is in the center of all the other questions. The questions in the secondary circles are the foundation questions that illuminate and help to clarify the essential question in the center. Thoughtfully developed essential questions are the linchpins of curriculum development. They guide the work that allows children to grow and achieve to their potential.

8. An effective Preview Learning curriculum will have differentiated strategies that link directly to the brain research on how learning occurs. The low achievers who are found in most regular classrooms really have no cap on their potential.

Figure 4.7   Preview Learning Program: Cluster Map—Essential Questions and Foundation Questions

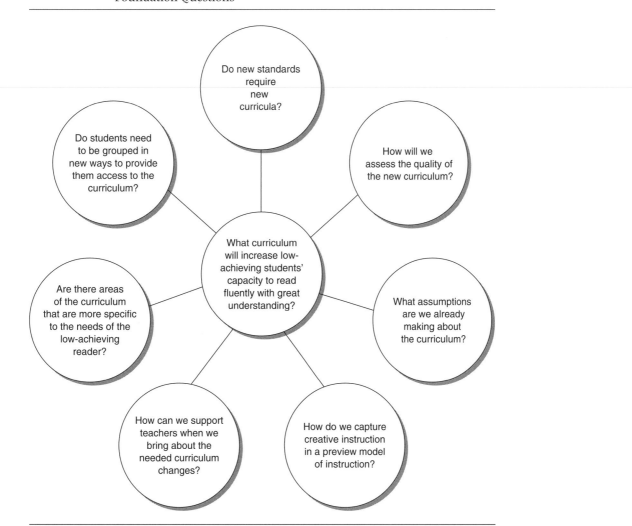

The rate and degree at which they learn differ. In reading, especially, some learn easily. Others do not. Marie Carbo writes: "If students do not learn in the way we teach them, we must teach them in the way that they learn." (Carbo, Dunn, & Dunn, 1986). Gregory and Chapman (2002) and Chapman and King (2003a) complement Carbo's statement by pointing out that teaching techniques and knowledge of content are of little use unless they are used "with the intent of honoring the diversity of the learners be it learning styles, multiple intelligences, or personal interests." Honoring those differences requires us to determine the growth edge for each child (especially the low achiever) and then meet each child at his or her unique achievement edge with a relevant curriculum and appropriate instructional strategies. Gregory and Chapman (2002) and Chapman and King (2003) call this *differentiation* and define it as meeting learners "where they are" in their unique abilities.

A differentiated reading curriculum, which addresses learning styles, multiple intelligences, and personal preferences, will appeal to the low achiever because:

- The student can be an active participant and not merely a passive learner. Reading is usually difficult for this type of child. Perhaps we know why! Sousa (2001) tells us, *"There are no areas of the brain that specialize in reading."* Wolfe and Nevills (2004) explain this further and address the two main processes in reading: decoding and comprehension. They explain how the brain shifts from the phonological processing in the angular gyrus and Wernicke's area to the higher-level comprehension skills, which are handled largely in Broca's area and the frontal lobe.

- The student will have the opportunity to experience the material through many senses, especially tactual and kinesthetic, which are frequently missing in the reading classroom. Sylwester (2000) indicates that reading must be explicitly taught, because we are dealing with the perceptual strengths that require connections in the brain that are abstract. This is why scaffolding works so well. It helps to build those connections. The curriculum-writing committee in William's district used scaffolding extensively for these very reasons.

- The student can experience success. *A teacher does not teach a class or group. He works with individuals who may be organized into teams, groups, or classes.* A person-centered, individualized approach to teaching reading will normally inspire a low achiever. Appropriate direct and explicit instruction can help the student caught in the achievement gap overcome nearly all deficits (Wolfe & Nevills, 2004). Numerous curriculum approaches, delivered in a variety of ways, will engage the learner and transform an ordinary day for a low achiever into an extraordinary event. William should have been blessed in such a way!

9. An effective Preview Learning curriculum will provide multiple opportunities for assessment. Throughout the day, a PLP must have built-in "touch points"— places where the teacher stops and checks for understanding and comprehension of the skill or concept that is being introduced. Even though the instruction is designed for awareness and not mastery, the student must feel a level of comfort and security with the new learning. Therefore, the teacher can use these touch points to monitor and adjust *what* to do next and determine *how* to present the information. The assessment should be formative and provide continuous feedback to ensure that the students learn more effectively (Chapman & King, 2005).

MAKING IT "LIVE" FOR YOU: A PLANNING TEMPLATE

1. Select qualified curriculum task force members to work together to plan any elements of the curriculum that the district needs to target for implementation of an intervention program. List your potential names here.

   _____
   _____
   _____
   _____

2. Conduct an initial brainstorming session on questions that the members of the task force may have about curriculum development. List your thoughts on a chart for easy reference.

3. Categorize the questions that you brainstormed by making a question wheel of your own, or use the question chart template in Worksheet 4.1 (see page 190 in the Resources). Use Figures 4.2, 4.3, and 4.4 to review the questioning process that is specific to the design process.

4. Determine if your state and district have written standards for the curriculum. If so, use your task force to decide how these standards will be applied in your curriculum development process.

5. Define your curriculum according to the information in this chapter.

6. Determine the skills and concepts at each grade level that will be taught in your intervention program. Rank-order them according to the *essential, important,* or *compact* criteria. Reminder: Your curriculum is being developed for preview purposes, not mastery.

7. Make your own cluster map using the template in Worksheet 4.2 (see page 191 in the Resources) to determine the essential and foundation questions for developing your Preview Learning Curriculum.

5

Value-Added Instruction

Start by doing what's necessary;
then do what's possible; and
suddenly you are doing the impossible.

—St. Francis of Assisi

INSTRUCTIONAL EFFECTIVENESS

Instruction matters! Effective instruction matters even more, especially for the students who are in need of skill building to correct deficit areas in reading. The word *effective* implies that correct strategies are being used to ensure that learning takes place, and that the teacher is working with a plan that reflects a knowledge and understanding of:

1. Reasoning processes that will help students understand the content of the curriculum

2. How to structure tasks that involve the use of knowledge—both procedural and declarative

3. How a skill or concept is acquired and integrated

4. How to apply strategies that make learning probable and forgetting less likely.

These four concepts are in alignment with Marzano's (2003) work on the power of the teacher-level factor on student achievement, and support an earlier reference in this book *What Teachers Should Know and Be Able to Do*, shown in Figure 3.1. In William's district, the Instructional Task Force (ITF) chose to develop an instructional model for the Preview Learning Program (PLP) that honors these significant thoughts.

MAKING CRITICAL DECISIONS

The task force members knew that they were enriching a standards-based program that was already in place, and they made four critical instructional decisions that can guide all of us in similar situations:

Critical Decision One: Focus all activities and learning experiences on the essential knowledge and "must-know" skills that are identified by the state's standardized blueprint for instruction and the district's curricula.

Critical Decision Two: Establish a structure for each day's teaching and learning.

Critical Decision Three: Use instructional activities that keep learners mentally active.

Critical Decision Four: Engage teachers in instructional decision making as a part of the lab-based professional growth activities.

ANALYZING THE CRITICAL DECISIONS

Critical Decision One. Focus all activities and learning experience on the essential knowledge and "must-know" skills that are identified by the state's standardized blueprint for instruction and the district's curricula.

The reading curriculum in William's district reflects its state's academic content standards. Value is added to these standards through a prioritization process of identifying the essential (E), important (I), and compact (C) concepts and skills (discussed in Chapter 4) for each grade level. In developing instructional strategies for daily lessons, the ITF will focus on the standards for each grade level that are *essential* for the next level of instruction. Two tasks, therefore, will be performed to accomplish this and meet the demands of this critical decision.

The first task is to review the essential reading skills for the first grading period for each grade level targeted in the Preview Learning Program, and then chart them for easy review. The lists for Grades 3 and 4 for the first six weeks of the regular school year reflect the work of the ITF and are shown in Figures 5.1 and 5.2.

Because good ideas can be implemented poorly, the next task that the instructional design group performed was to transplant their ideas into practice. They developed a rubric to help them create effective lessons with strong instructional strategies designed to help students in the achievement gap acquire the needed skills. The rubric is an instructional assistance that will guide the group's thinking, keep the instruction from being textbook-driven,

Figure 5.1   Standards-Based Essential Academic Skills Introduced in Grading Period One, Preview Learning Program Grade Three

- Sequencing the events in a story (E)
- Making appropriate inferences from text (E)
- Identifying setting, characters, and plot (E)
- Understanding basic plot features of short stories and folk tales (E)
- Rereading to find details (E)
- Knowing grade-level compound words, contractions, common abbreviations, and vowel digraphs (E)
- Decoding multisyllabic words (E)
- Completing a simple graphic organizer to group ideas for writing (E)
- Correctly using nouns, verbs, and adjectives within context (E)
- Writing in response to a narrative prompt (E)
- Spelling appropriate words correctly (E)

E = essential skill; I = important skill; C = compact skill

Figure 5.2   Standards-Based Essential Academic Skills Introduced in Grading Period One, Preview Learning Program Grade Four

- Relating plot, setting, and characters to own experiences and ideas (E)
- Knowing appropriate synonyms, antonyms, and homonyms within context (E)
- Summarizing major points from text and discussions (E)
- Identifying character, setting, and plot of story (E)
- Completing a graphic organizer to group ideas for writing (E)
- Making predictions, sequencing ideas, and making inferences by referencing the text (E)
- Decoding multisyllabic words (E)
- Identifying key words and discovering meanings (E)
- Writing simple and compound sentences, and avoiding fragments and run-on sentences (E)
- Applying phonetic strategies to reading and writing new words (E)
- Understanding the difference between fact, fiction, and opinion (E)
- Listening to follow multiple directions (E)

E = essential skill; I = important skill; C = compact skill

and provide a framework for lesson development for the Preview Learning Program. The program's goal mandates instructional strategies that encourage high achievement beginning with the student's earliest contact with the program, so having a proven method for planning effective lessons that focus on student learning is critical.

The rubric (see Figure 5.3) is general in design and specific only to the awareness level of instruction, since that is the focus of the PLP. It will guide the actual development, however, of the daily lessons. The rubric also incorporates

Figure 5.3 Rubric Designing an Effective Acquisition Lesson

One	The instructional design is mostly driven by the textbook and makes use of only one instructional strategy.
Two	The instruction uses an essential question to guide learning, has an activating strategy, is mostly driven by the textbook, and makes use of one additional instructional strategy.
Three	The instruction uses an essential question to guide learning, has an activating and closing strategy, and uses an organizational tool and one additional instructional strategy.
Four	The instruction is standards-based, uses an essential question to guide learning, has an activating and closing strategy, uses an organizational tool, includes opportunities for distributed practice and work in collaborative pairs, uses one additional instructional strategy to diversify instruction, and includes teacher modeling using a "think-aloud" process.

the thinking of Max Thompson, Learning Concepts, Inc., and his teaching on Level One of learning-focused instruction, the acquisition level. (Level Two, *extending and refining,* and Level Three, *authentic use and mastery,* of Dr. Thompson's work are excellent platforms to incorporate in the year's regular curriculum to advance the skills of the students who have participated in the Preview Learning Program.)

Critical Decision Two. Establish a structure for each day's teaching and learning.

A lesson structure will encourage teachers' confidence in their ability to adapt effective lessons and strategies. Its form should be a plan that works within the teacher's time and capacity to implement it, and provide a variety of instructional approaches and techniques. Using full knowledge of all the implications of an acquisition lesson (see Figure 5.4), the ITF and lesson writing team reviewed the categories and decided which ones to include in the lesson design for the PLP. The design they chose will include all the elements shown in Figure 5.5. Brain breaks are built in to include movements that express knowledge and facilitate greater cognitive function. Movement is effective with many students—and even adults—to anchor thought and build *essential* skills (Hannaford, 1995). In the district's design, distributed practice is mixed throughout the instruction to give students an opportunity to periodically summarize what they have learned, and to give teachers a chance to informally assess students' level of understanding of the new information.

THE ACQUISITION LESSON

Planning the Lesson

The Acquisition Lesson Planning Form, displayed in Figure 5.6, provides a structure to guide the thinking process of the design team in William's district as they create daily lessons for the PLP.

Figure 5.4   Acquisition: Definition

- Acquiring new information, new concepts, new skills
- Linking new knowledge to prior knowledge
- Creating meaning from new knowledge
- Organizing new information in short-term and long-term memory
- Storing new information in short-term and long-term memory
- Expanding vocabulary in the context of new knowledge
- Applying and shaping skills through distributed guided practice and multiple opportunities for feedback
- Internalizing skills through massed practice and the meaningful use of knowledge

SOURCE: *Learning Concepts, Inc. (2005). Used by permission.*

Figure 5.5   Acquisition: Lesson Design

PREVIEW LEARNING PROGRAM (Acquiring New Skills and Knowledge)

- Standard, blueprint for learning, or essential skill
- Essential question of lesson
- Activating thinking: Relating to student's experience, building on prior knowledge, keeping learner mentally active
- Cognitive teaching strategies: More than one way to learn within the lesson; distributed, guided practice, summarizing in pairs for formative assessment, visualizing and organizing, questioning, brain breaks for shaping and internalizing
- Summarizing strategies: Learning individually and in collaborative pairs summarizing and answering questions
- Assessment: Reciprocal teaching, interviewing, oral retelling, writing, answering essential question, portfolio selection, and teacher conferencing

The Literacy Instructional Framework

Many at-risk students benefit when instruction provides a diverse set of experiences to help them learn. It is always important to address a range of strengths! In this intervention program, students stay mentally active and build on their growth edge through an instructional framework that is particularly effective for teaching that portion of the curriculum that is taught for awareness only. Each element of the framework (Figure 5.7) will be explicitly taught for at least 40 minutes a day throughout the four-week program. Word study, guided reading, skills and language, and writing make up the four strands of this literacy program. The strands are thoughtfully integrated, reinforce each other, and include opportunities for specific skill development in print concepts, phonemic awareness, phonics, word structures, and word attack skills to be taught in a systematic manner.

Figure 5.6   Acquisition: Lesson Planning Form

Preview Learning Program

Supplies and Materials:

| Grade: |
| Week: |
| Day: |
| Strand: |

....

1. **Standard, blueprint for learning, or target skills:**
   - Topic or focus of the learning stated in simple phrases

....

2. **Essential question:**
   - What should students know and be able to do at the end of the lesson?

....

3. **Activating thinking strategies: Learners are mentally active.**

Beginning of the Lesson (Part One)

- Link to prior knowledge
- Motivate or "grab" the learner's interest
- Set goal for the lesson with essential question

....

4. **Cognitive teaching strategies:**

Middle of the Lesson (Part Two)

Declarative Content	**Procedural Content**
Learner constructs meaning, organizes information, and stores and remembers information.	Learner "sees" how to do skills, applies and shapes skills, and internalizes skills through practice.

- Moving toward acquisition of knowledge
- Brain break for shaping and internalizing
- Guided practice for monitoring, clarifying learning, and reteaching
- Formative assessment to continually improve instruction and learning

....

5. **Revisit essential question and summarize:**

End of the Lesson (Part Three)

- Learner summarizes, summarizes, summarizes, individually and in pairs
- Learner answers the essential question

....

6. **Assessment:**
   - Offer choices
   - Portfolio selection and teacher conferencing

SOURCE: Adapted from Acquisition Lesson Planning, *Learning Focused Strategies Notebook*, Learning Concepts, 2005.

Figure 5.7   Acquisition: Literacy Instructional Framework

Preview Learning Program

Word Study Strand • Phonics and phonemic awareness • Vocabulary • Word building • Structural skills • Letter and sound manipulation	**Guided Reading Strand** • Concepts of print • Story organization • Author's purpose • Genre • Fluency
Skills and Language Strand • Targeted comprehension skills • Reading response • Metacognition • Retelling and summarizing • Structure of language	**Writing Strand** • Guided writing • Interactive writing • Independent writing • Reading response journals • Focused process writing

Sample Acquisition Lesson

Acquisition activities should engage the learner in a meaningful way. Activating prior knowledge, summarizing the lesson, talking about similarities and differences, using covert thinking to precede overt responses, working in collaborative pairs, using distributed practice, and inviting students to assess their own progress daily are only a few of the activities that the PLP uses to help the *gap student* learn and remember. These strategies and others provide a scaffold for student learning (Boyles, 2005) and are included in all the acquisition lessons used in the PLP. One sample lesson (see Figure 5.8 and all its subparts: 5.8a, 5.8b, 5.8c, 5.8d, 5.8e, 5.8f, and 5.8g) for Grade 4 is included in its entirety to illustrate the four strands, show the alignment between the strands, and present a picture of the depth of a day's work for the teacher and the student. All grades (Grades 2–5) in the PLP have the same lesson structure. Note that all the strands identified in Figure 5.7 are included in the following lessons.

After reviewing the four strands and the sample lessons for each strand it is important to note:

- E. D. Hirsch, Jr. (1987) proposes ". . . vocabulary instruction as an effective means for imparting that portion of the curriculum that would not be taught in depth." Teaching vocabulary in a systematic way is a powerful strategy for raising student achievement.
- The most critical aspect of cognitive strategy instruction is teacher modeling. McEwan (2004) says that it is important to think aloud so that students can observe exactly how to use this strategy to become skilled readers.

(*Text continues on page 76*)

Figure 5.8a   Acquisition Lesson: Word Study

Materials and Supplies: Vocabulary words on color-coded strips of paper; chart stand; chart tablet; colored marker; utility ball to bounce per child, borrowed from the physical education department; students' KnowBook*

Grade 4
Week 2
Day 1
Word
Study

....

1. **Target Skills:**
   - Building new vocabulary words
   - Listening for syllables in a word
   - Learning the meanings of words

....

2. **Essential Question:**
   - How can words help us make a picture in our minds of unknown places?

....

3. **Vocabulary Words:**

   - majestic
   - breathtaking
   - eucalyptus (n)
   - emerge
   - rain forest
   - abruptly
   - koala (n)
   - bellow
   - Bunya Mountains (n)
   - kookaburra (n)
   - countryside

....

4. **Activating Learning:**

   Teacher Talk: Think about a time when you may have taken a ride to the mountains with your parents, other family members, or a friend. If you haven't taken a trip like that, think about a program that you have watched on TV where mountains could be seen. Now, close your eyes and recall pictures of the things that you saw in the mountains. (Pause) Make sure that you see the things in "living color." Keeping your eyes closed, listen for sounds in the same mountains. Maybe some of the things that you are seeing in your mind are making the sounds. Maybe the sounds are coming from things that you cannot see in your mind. Open your eyes. Take your pencil and your KnowBook* and spend only two minutes drawing some of the things that you "saw."

   Teacher Talk: I'm going to write words in a list of what you "saw." I'll take one word at a time beginning with the person on my left. As I continue to go around the circle, you will pick one word to give me that someone else has not already given. If it is your turn, and you have already given me all your words, simply say "Pass." Let's begin with the first word, please.

   Teacher Do: Draw a large "T" on the chart. List the "see" words on the left side of the T.

   Teacher Talk: Repeat the same directions you used for the "see" words, but reframe it for what they "heard." (They only have the covert experience to rely on here, so their ideas may be a little scattered.)

   Teacher Do: List the words for the "heard" sounds on the right side of the T.

   Teacher Talk: Today we are going to read about some special mountains in Australia. The characters in our story are going on a trip to the mountains. They will see special sights that may be like the sights that you saw, but some of the sights may be different from yours. On the trip to the mountains in this story, we will "listen" for sounds in their mountains and see if they are like any of the sounds that we heard during our imaginary trip.

....

5. **Cognitive Teaching:**

   Explicit Vocabulary Instruction and Guided Practice: (Show the 11 vocabulary words that you have previously written on individual sentence strips and attached to the chart tablet with double-stick tape. The four words above with an (n) after them should be written on one color strip that is common to the four, and the remaining seven on another color strip.

Teacher Talk: The seven words that you see on the "white" strips are words that we learned last week. They will continue to be in our story today. Let's review them by having you go to the chart and select *one* word that will answer our "question of the minute." Take your choice of answer off the chart and place it on the tray. More than one of you may have to go to the chart if there is more than one answer to the question. Find a compound word; a word that will complete this sentence: "A synonym of *grand* is _____."; a sound word; a word that shows movement; a word that has a silent letter; a word that comes after *bellow* if we arrange them in alphabetical order.

Collaborative Sharing: Turn to your "partner of the week." Make up a sentence using one of the "old" words and tell it to your partner. When you have completed this activity, both of you will have shared. The person wearing the most of one color will go first. I will listen to your sentences as you share with each other. Begin, please.

Teacher Talk with Modeling: There are four new vocabulary words in our story today. (Use the following process with each word.)

1. Say the entire word. Repeat word and clap your hands for each syllable as you say it.
   Bun • ya   Moun • tains
   Use the word in a sentence. Say, "I'm going to make up a sentence using the new word and I'm going to try to use one of the words from our vocabulary list of previous words if I can find some that make sense with my sentence."
   "The majestic Bunya Mountains have a rain forest with walking trails."

2. I'm going to repeat what I just did, but now I need you to help me when I invite you to talk by putting my hand out in front of me with my palm up and stop talking.
   "The words Bun-ya Moun-tains have more than one syllable. The number of syllables that we hear are (4)."
   "The Bun-ya Moun-tains are _____. In the mountains we can walk on _____in the rain forest."

3. Let's do this one more time and I'll help you if you want me to, just the way you helped me.
   Say *Bun ya Moun tains* three times, clapping your hands with each part of the word.

4. Turn to your "partner of the week" and when I say, "Begin," say *Bun ya Moun tains* and use the new word in a sentence that will give your partner a picture in his mind of the Bunya Mountains. Think about your sentence. Begin telling your partner.

Continue this process with the other three words. To help you construct meaningful sentences, you may want to use the following information:

❖ Kookaburra – laughing bird; says "kook-kook-kook" when it starts laughing and ends the laughing with a "ha-ha-ha;" not a good flyer; family groups laugh together.
❖ Eucalyptus – a tree of Australia. The leaves are 50 percent to 75 percent water, depending on the time of year.
❖ Koala – fussy eater; eats 50 different types of eucalyptus leaves; sleeps about 19 hours a day; not a bear; lives in eastern Australia.

....

Brain Break: Give each student a utility ball to bounce with instructions to say each of the four new words three times each while bouncing the ball one time for each syllable.

....

Summarizing and Assessment: Essential Question Revisited:
Stand and stroll with your "partner of the week." One partner explains to the other about a picture that was "painted" in his mind by using a new vocabulary word. The other partner will share one "picture" that is in his head that he "drew" from using the new vocabulary words.

Teacher will monitor the sharing time for assessment. Remember, this is for awareness only, not mastery.

NOTE: *KnowBook is a term used by Rob Abernathy and Mark Reardon in *Hot Tips for Facilitators: Strategies to Make Life Easier for Anyone Who Leads, Guides, Teaches, or Trains Groups* (2003).

Figure 5.8b   Acquisition Lesson: Guided Reading and Comprehension

---

Materials and Supplies: Story, *Kippy Koala Goes to the Bunya Mountains*; Prediction Poster

Grade 4
Week 2
Day 1
Guided
Reading and
Comprehension

....

1. **Target Skills:** • Fact, fiction, and opinion
                       • Predicting

....

2. **Essential Question:**
                          • What information in the story of Kippy Koala could actually happen?

....

3. **Activating Learning:** (Do *not* give students a copy of the story at this time.) Show the story to the students and read its full title: *Kippy Koala Goes to the Bunya Mountains*; author, Marti Richardson; illustrator, Ima Computer.

   ❖ Explain that this story tells about a trip that was taken by Kippy Koala to the Bunya Mountains.

   ❖ Model predicting by saying and showing the poster that reads: *"When I predict, I tell in advance what I think will happen in the story by using clues from the words that I have been studying and by looking at the pictures in the story. The title helps me predict, also."* See Figure 5.8c.

Prediction	Chart
Pictures	Words

   ❖ Ask students to share predictions that they make by looking at the pictures and word clues. Record predictions on a "T" chart under the appropriate columns, labeled picture and word clues

....

4. **Cognitive Teaching:** (Distribute a copy of the story to each child)

   Teacher Talk: Invite the students to read the first two paragraphs of the story silently to find out

   ❖ Who suggested that Kippy would like to go to the Bunya Mountains?

   ❖ What is one special event that takes place daily in the Bunya Mountains?

   ❖ What is the name of Kippy's friend?

   Discuss answers. Have students share-read the paragraphs orally with their "partner of the week." Paragraph two: Read to find out

   ❖ What worried Kippy about the trip?
   ❖ What decision did Kippy make?

   Follow the same procedure as with paragraphs one and two. Have students make a prediction before silently reading paragraph three.

   ❖ What do you think that Kippy packed in his lunch?

Read paragraph three to see if the prediction is true and to see why taking a lunch was an important thing for Kippy to do. Discuss.

Paragraph four. Read to find out

❖ How did Kippy make his way through the Bunya Mountains?

Paragraph five. Read to be able to describe the scene at the picnic.
Predict before paragraph six:

❖ What do you think has emerged that is troubling to Kippy? Read to find out if what you thought is true.

Paragraph seven. Read to find out

❖ Why was it hard for Kippy to make the trip to the Bunya Mountains?
....

Brain Break: Sometimes koalas will leave the trees if there is no other way to reach a new food tree or if they want to drink water from a stream. They aren't comfortable on the ground and they walk on all four legs with an awkward, swaying motion. Explain this to the students and have them imitate a koala walking by doing a "koala walk" around the room.
....

5. **Summarizing and Essential Question Revisited:** Orally retell the story with the students by giving sentence stems to cue their thinking. Take their responses in a round-robin circle—that is, one at a time as you go around the circle. Suggested sentence stems include:

❖ Kippy's parents told him the Bunya Mountains had _____.

❖ Kippy took a lunch with him because _____.

❖ It was special that Kippy took his lunch because _____.

❖ To get through the Bunya Mountains, Kippy _____.

❖ The picnic area _____.

❖ The picnic area ____ *(keep repeating this prompt until the story has been sufficiently summarized)*.

❖ Kippy was glad _____.

❖ The information in this story that is a *fact* includes _____.

❖ The information in this story that is *fiction* is _____.

❖ Something that we have discussed today that is *opinion* includes _____.

6. **Assessment:** Teacher observation of oral responses to completion of sentence stems.

Figure 5.8c   Acquisition Lesson: Prediction

Prediction

When I predict, I tell in advance

what I think

will happen in the story

by using clues

from the words that I have

been studying

and by looking at the pictures

in the story.

The title helps me predict, also!

Figure 5.8d   Acquisition Lesson: Skills and Language

Materials and Supplies: Sticky notes; colored paper; overhead projector; overhead transparency and transparency pen	**Grade 4** **Week 2** **Day 1** **Skills and** **Language**

....

1. **Target Skills:** • Sequencing
   • Completing a graphic organizer to group ideas for writing.

....

2. **Essential Question:**
   • How does ordering the events in the story help us understand the story?

....

3. **Activating Learning:**
   Teacher Talk: Think back to this morning when you woke up. What was the first thing you did? Next after that? Next? (Work on an overhead transparency and list the responses of an individual student in vertically placed, rectangular boxes.) We have just written your answers in the order that they occurred. That is called *sequence*. When we write the responses in boxes like we have just done and connect the boxes with lines we make a flow chart. A flow chart helps us see how each part of the story is connected. One strategy that can be used to put information from a story in sequence is to find the first and last event, and then try filling in the events that happened in the middle.

4. **Cognitive Teaching:**
   Visualizing and Organizing and Distributed Practice:
   Teacher Talk:

   ❖ Let's go back to our four new vocabulary words that we had earlier in the morning. I have four sticky notes for each of you. Each of the sticky notes has one of the new words written on it. Place the notes in order on the colored sheet of paper that I'm giving you to indicate the order in which they were used in the story. When you are sure that you have the words in correct sequence mash them to the paper good with your thumbs, then take your pencil and connect the notes together by drawing connecting lines between the notes.

Koala	**Bunya Mountains**	**eucalyptus**	**kookaburra**

   You have made a flow chart.

   ❖ Write a sentence below each note that includes the word on the note above it *and* the word you see on the note to the right of the word of choice. When you get to the last word, use the first word to pair with it.

(Continued)

Figure 5.8d (Continued)

Brain Break: Stand and sequence yourselves in a line to show the order of your birthdays.

··

5. Summarizing:

❖ Pair-share with your "partner of the week" and read the sentences that you wrote.
❖ Pair-share with your partner the answer to the Essential Question, *"How does ordering the events in the story help us to understand the story?"*

6. Assessment:

❖ Teacher monitors original sentences and answers to Essential Question. Prompt and cue for more thorough answers in a follow-up discussion, if necessary.
❖ Have students write at the top of their flow chart this sentence stem:
  ○ "My flow chart shows _____."
  Date the work and place the flow chart in the student's portfolio.

- Scaffolding is built into the acquisition lesson design. It is a planned withdrawal of support for the student, to help the student learn to work independently. If scaffolding is maintained too long, it becomes a crutch.
- A running commentary by teachers will help at-risk students gradually become self-regulated and cognitively competent.
- Whenever students like William are expected to extract and construct meaning from words, the teacher should model, explain, scaffold, and coach as teaching strategies are used (Boyles, 2005; McEwan, 2004).
- There are specific instructional methods that produce results to teach cognitive strategies to students. The PLP uses these instructional methods daily.
- An activating lesson design promotes learning because it incorporates the recall of relevant prior knowledge and experiences from long-term memory. That recall helps the learner construct meaning from new, related material.
- Max Thompson (Learning Concepts, Inc.) gives two characteristics of a Preview Learning Lesson. The PLP honors both.
  ○ Vocabulary is explicitly taught before the lesson and in context during the lesson.
  ○ Advance organizers (concept maps, story maps, visual tools) are used to help construct knowledge and communicate that knowledge to others.

(Text continues on page 80)

Figure 5.8e   Acquisition Lesson: Writing

Materials and Supplies: Student paper and pencil; overhead projector; transparency film and marker; student portfolios; blank Bubble Maps (2). See Figure 5.8f.

| Grade 4 |
| Week 2 |
| Day 1 |
| Writing |

....

1. **Target Skills:**   • Using a graphic organizer to group ideas for writing
   • Identifying attributes

....

2. **Essential Question:**
   • How do thinking maps help us organize our writing?

....

3. **Activating Learning:** We read about Kippy and the Bunya Mountains in our story. While reading, we learned several things about each. We're going to make a Bubble Map*** about Kippy to help us more easily see his characteristics. Because you know how to do a Flow Chart, a Bubble Map will be easy to do.

....

4. **Cognitive Teaching:**

   Teacher Modeling: Visualizing and Organizing

   Teacher Talk: I'm going to give you the words from the story and some other activities that we did this morning that describe what we know about Kippy.

   Teacher Modeling – Step One: I will draw a shape in the center of my transparency and add other shapes as I identify each characteristic for Kippy. The name, Kippy Koala, will go in the center shape. Words that give characteristics about Kippy will be put in the outer shapes. (Use a diagram similar to Figure 5.8f on the transparency machine. Put the appropriate words in the boxes.) Insert phrases much like these in the outer shapes. Say each out loud as you write it: *fussy eater; happy; leaps from tree to tree; uneasy about food; eats only eucalyptus leaves; took a lunch; sleeps nineteen hours a day; selects only good leaves; has low energy – rests a lot; body made for climbing; doesn't need water; hard for him to walk.*

   Teacher Modeling – Step Two: It's your time to help me. We'll do the Bubble Map again and you are invited to see how many of the characteristics that you recall from what I've just done. You tell me the characteristics that you can remember and I'll write them in their special shape. I'll help with clues if I need to.

   Teacher Modeling – Step Three: (Pass out a blank Bubble Map to students.) It's time for me to help you do a Bubble Map on paper. We'll follow the same procedure that we used just now in step two but this time you say the characteristic in turn and we'll both write it down. You may use the words I write on the transparency to help you, if you would like.

   Teacher Modeling – Step Four: Now you get to make a Bubble Map on your own. You may choose to make another map on Kippy or you may choose to make one on the Bunya Mountains. Whichever map you choose to make, use the words on the Word Wall and the vocabulary chart to help you spell the tricky words. (Phrases for Bunya Mountains may include: *walking tracks; majestic; pine trees; eucalyptus trees; "alive"; daily feeding; picnic area; king parrots; other birds.*

(Continued)

Figure 5.8e   (Continued)

Brain Break: Stand where you are and sway like a eucalyptus tree that has a koala moving in its branches to jump to another tree.

....

5. **Summarizing:** Use the following sentence stems and have students write the sentences using the Bubble Map to complete their thoughts.

   ❖ Kippy eats _____ and is _____.
   ❖ Kippy doesn't _____.
   ❖ With a body made for climbing, Kippy _____.
   ❖ Kippy likes _____ and has _____.

6. **Assessment:**

   ❖ Read the sentences in a pair-share. Teacher monitor. Place sentences in students' portfolios with the current date written on the paper.
   ❖ Revisit Essential Question. How did using the Bubble Map help you organize your answers to complete the sentences and make decisions about what words to put in the blanks?

NOTE: ***The term Bubble Map is a term used by David Hyerle for students to use to describe characteristics. It is explained in Hyerle (1996, p. 101).

Figure 5.8f   Acquisition Lesson: Lesson Map

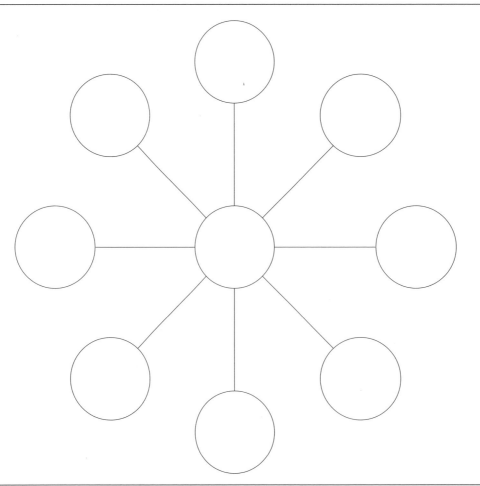

Figure 5.8g   Acquisition Lesson: Story

Kippy Koala Goes to the Bunya Mountains
Author: Marti Richardson   Illustrator: Ima Computer

Kippy Koala wanted to take a trip to the mountains. In the month of September (when it was just getting springtime warm) he decided it was a good time to go. His parents had told him about the Bunya Mountains and how there were walking trails for people and plenty of eucalyptus trees for koalas. There were also many pine trees and a picnic area. He learned from his father that the Bunya Mountains has a daily feeding at the picnic area for the king parrots and other birds. He wanted to be there for the picnic and see the king parrots eat. Perhaps he would also see Laughing Kookaburra, his good friend. Laughing liked picnics, too.

Kippy was happy that he would have food to eat when he got to the Bunya Mountains. Since there are many eucalyptus trees he knew that was the only food and water that he needed. The thing that caused him to be a little uneasy was what he would eat while he was on the flat countryside before he got to the mountains and its rain forest. He decided to take a lunch with him.

Kippy's lunch had only one thing—eucalyptus leaves! He had carefully sniffed each leaf to help him decide if it was a leaf that was fit to eat. If it hadn't smelled exactly right, Kippy would have passed it by. It was a good thing that his body was made for climbing around in trees. His special body helped him get to enough eucalyptus leaves to select just the right ones for his lunch. There would be no need to take water, because the leaves would give him all the water he needed.

He wasn't happy making his trip on the ground of the flat countryside. It was very hard for him to walk and he was glad when he saw several eucalyptus trees. He happily climbed the first one by using his sharp claws and then leaped through the air to the second and third trees. When Kippy stopped at the third tree he

became excited that he had packed his lunch. This eucalyptus tree didn't have the kind of leaves that he liked. After all, Kippy is a very fussy eater! Kippy ate the lunch that he packed and continued his journey to the picnic area by, once again, leaping from tree to tree.

The picnic area at the Bunya Mountains was full of people and birds. The king parrots were eating seeds from the hands of the people (who had bought food to feed the parrots from a small, nearby stand) as well as eating the food on the ground that has fallen from the people's picnic lunches. Some of the parrots had bad manners and sat on the shoulders or heads of the people. It was a breathtaking scene for Kippy. The majestic Bunya Mountains were "alive" for Kippy to see. But wait! Something has emerged that is troubling to the people. It has happened abruptly!

In a tree close to Kippy is Laughing Kookaburra. Laughing hasn't been invited to the picnic and he is sitting on a pine tree branch laughing, *Kook-Kook-Kook* and ending with *Ha-Ha-Ha*. The laughing sound that has emerged for all to hear is worse than a bellow. Kippy knows Laughing and understands that his *Kook-Kook-Kook, Ha-Ha-Ha* is the way that Laughing has of telling everyone that he feels left out of the picnic. He doesn't eat bird seeds and that is all that he sees for food at the picnic. He wants insects, snails, and worms for his picnic. There is none available, but Kippy is glad to see Laughing all the same. The people at the picnic area are not happy to see Kookaburra, however, because his laughing scared them.

Kippy made his way home after the picnic at the Bunya Mountains. It had been an exciting day but he wasn't eager to repeat this type of activity often. It is very hard for a koala that sleeps about 19 hours a day to go to the rain forest and stay up all day. He was very tired! It will be a long time before he makes the trip again because he must rest and regain his energy.

- Two graphic organizers are good. More than two are even better! More than two will notch up student achievement. The acquisition lesson design in the Preview Learning Program uses more than two. This is important for at-risk students, because graphic organizers allow them to see their thinking (Gregory & Chapman, 2002).
- Essential questions are tools for the teacher to use to gather evidence of learning. Thompson says that there may be several key questions under an essential question, but there is only one essential question.

Critical Decision Three. Use instructional activities that keep learners mentally active.

The core concern of this meaningful decision by William's district revolves around the quality of instruction that the students in the PLP receive. It is critical for students who are caught in the achievement gap to have a *short-term win!* Therefore, the program must focus on instructing for success. This occurs when there is active teaching and learning and the instruction is assessment-driven.

Active teaching and learning: We know that students learn more when they are actively engaged in instructional activities. In the PLP the students are engaged in more activities, not less, with the idea that the multiple activities will give the student a greater potential for learning. The instructional activities used to teach content and keep learners mentally active in the Preview Learning Program include:

- Numbered heads
- Essential questions
- Prompts
- Know/want to know/learned
- KWL plus
- Word wall
- Writing to inform
- Frayer Model
- Chunking
- Guided reading
- Distributed practice
- The sequence chart
- 5 W Model
- Prediction tree
- Collaborative pairs

- Cognitive web
- Flow map
- Bubble map
- Bridge map
- Circle map
- Multiflow map
- Compare/Contrast diagram
- Fishbone
- Story map
- Matrix
- T-Chart
- PMI
- KnowBook
- Thinking at right angles
- Word sort

Added to the instructional activities in the Preview Learning Program, which are listed above, are instructional strategies that McEwan (2004) identifies as strategies used by *effective* readers:

- Activating
- Inferring
- Monitoring–clarifying

- Searching–selecting
- Summarizing
- Visualizing–organizing

McEwan (2004) tells us that each of these activities is backed by research evidence.

Assessment-driven instruction: Since the Preview Learning Program is an awareness program, it is important for students to develop a skill of self-monitoring so that they may become more independent, self-regulated learners. Therefore, students will keep a KnowBook and a portfolio of their work. Fluency tapes for each child will give immediate feedback and reinforcement for the student's progress to date. Cooperative learning and partner work will allow students to learn from one another.

Critical Decision Four. Engage teachers in instructional decision making as a part of the lab-based professional growth activities.

This decision is addressed more thoroughly in Chapter 6, because of its importance to the success of the students as related to their learning. Time will be built into the schedule in the district to make it possible for the program's teachers to:

- Have the opportunity to respond to ground-level complexities that happen on a day-to-day basis
- Have recurrent opportunities to examine the students' work and assessment results for the purpose of revising the instructional strategies and planned curriculum

Through collaboration in the lab-based program, the practitioners will have ample opportunity to answer the questions, *"Why did that strategy work with the students?"* or *"What went wrong with that instructional strategy?"*

MAKING IT "LIVE" FOR YOU: A PLANNING TEMPLATE

1. The instructional design team in William's district chose to develop an *instructional model* for their Preview Learning Program that reflected their understanding of the way students learn in specific situations. Activities were tailored to match the approach and enhance the probability that students will learn. Four critical decisions were made by the district based on this understanding. Use those decisions to assist you in building your template.
   - Review your knowledge about instruction and determine how your understanding and recent research of the words *effective instruction* can be used as a springboard to enrich the instructional paradigm in

your district—especially in the way instruction is organized and delivered for the at-risk student.

- Use the visual aid, Worksheet 5.1 (see page 192 in the Resources), to help you "see" your thinking.

2. Review the academic content standards for your state and district. Prioritize the standards as *essential (E), important (I),* or *compact (C)* concepts and skills for each grade level. In a Preview Learning Program, it is important to focus your attention on the concepts and skills in each grade that are *essential* for the next level of instruction. Since the focus of this book is reading, Worksheet 5.2 (see page 193 in the Resources) is provided as a subject-specific organizer for you to use. The visual aid is general enough, however, to be used for all subjects and grade levels when prioritizing content standards for E's, I's, and C's.

- The chart you developed in Worksheet 5.2 may be further expanded to identify the grading period in which each of the prioritized concepts and skills will be taught. Worksheet 5.3 (see page 194 in the Resources) will assist you in completing the expansion process.

3. Develop a rubric to help you create effective acquisition lessons. You may use the one shown in Figure 5.3 or develop one that is more specific to your needs. Thompson and Thomason (1998) explain in a video from *The Video Journal of Education* the five steps of developing a rubric. Listed here as four "D's" and one "S," they are:

D etermine the focus of instruction.

D ecide the number of categories.

D escribe the elements (actions, processes, and attitudes) needed to reach the highest level of performance.

D etermine the number of levels appropriate to move along a continuum from 1 (low) to your highest level.

S elect the presentation format of the rubric.

4. Develop your literacy instructional framework for acquisition learning. Review Figure 5.7 and then determine the strands that will be used in your district. Worksheet 5.4 (see page 195 in the Resources) is provided to help you in this activity.

5. Develop acquisition lessons. Review Figures 5.6 and 5.8a–5.8g for a structure to guide you in your thinking process and creative action. Include instructional activities to keep the learners mentally active.

6. Explore your thinking on formative assessment. Identify at least three things that you can do daily to keep both you and students current on the status of their learning.

- _____

- _____

- _____

7. Determine what teachers must know and be able to do to make your instructional plan come alive. Write down the ideas that you generate. Chapter 6 will give you research-based implementation strategies and critical formats, which you may use to apply your ideas. Using each of the strategies and formats will help to ensure success for both the teacher and the students.

6

Professional Development for Student Learning

*I am confident that content and topic-specific
staff development is essential.*

—Lee Shulman, Professor
School of Education, Stanford University

FINDING THE KEY TO SUCCESS

The key to success in bridging the achievement gap is the professional growth of educators, because teacher effectiveness is not a fixed entity. To be effective, one needs continual development of conceptual understanding in order to use appropriate strategies with students in the classroom. There are many well-known adversities that beset youngsters in the gap. The odds are often stacked against these children, but teachers and administrators who have a passion to learn, and a powerful intention to change the base learning behavior of these students, can breathe new life into their achievement level.

Teachers are not born knowing how to teach reading, the subject that is the focus of the Preview Learning Program (PLP) in William's district, nor do they inherently know the relationships among the basic skills of reading and reading comprehension. When children like those in the achievement gap read poorly, it may not be obvious that the youngsters must be *taught basic reading skills* before they can make progress. Stein (1993) says that a child cannot understand what he cannot decode, but what he does decode will be meaningless unless he can understand it. Therefore, teachers must skillfully teach linguistics, awareness, and phonics while linking the skills to context as much as possible. The fact that teachers need training to carry out this deliberate instruction is a call for action. That action includes the type of staff development that assists teachers in developing the knowledge and skills that are inherent in effective reading. Teaching reading correctly must be in a teacher's reading instructional repertoire. It is a necessity in a Preview Learning Program!

If teachers have not been exposed to research-based knowledge in reading instruction, this can serve as the basis for content-based staff development. Content-based staff development was the choice of the Instructional Task Force (ITF) in William's district. Their program design is organized around four components of reading instruction that form a core curriculum for teacher preparation: developing an understanding of reading development; reviewing the structure of the English language; knowing how to apply best practices in reading instruction; and exploring how to use reliable and efficient assessment to inform their classroom instruction.

SETTING THE STANDARD FOR PROFESSIONAL LEARNING IN THE PROGRAM

A program of professional growth for teachers must focus on improving student achievement. The planning to date in William's district has acknowledged this concept, and the design team is ready to move ahead in their program development. Since the student learning data have already been studied, the team is ready to examine those standards that should guide the planning for professional growth opportunities.

The National Staff Development Council (NSDC) created staff development standards, with the assistance of representation from most major content organizations, in 1994. In 2001, the standards were revised for more effective use in the field. The ITF in William's district uses these standards as their road map (Mizell, 2001) to develop the professional growth component of the lab-based PLP, because

- A standards-based professional development program is critical to ensuring that teachers develop appropriate understandings and skills and learn how to translate research into classroom practice (Gaddy, Dean, & Kendall, 2002).
- Students are now being held to high standards; therefore, they need teachers who know the subject and how to teach it (Haycock, 2001a).
- Many researchers in a variety of disciplines have demonstrated empirically how standards affect personal *and* organizational effectiveness (Kouzes & Posner, 1993).
- Previous professional development activities in William's district have been unfocused, and follow-up to achieve results was missing.

STUDENT SUCCESS AND THE STANDARDS

Standards-based professional development will ensure that more students learn! In the area of reading, scientists now estimate that 95 percent of all children can be taught to read at "a level constrained only by their reasoning and listening comprehension abilities" (Fletcher & Lyon, 1998). To reach that level of achievement, we must take what Margaret Wheatley (Wheatley & Kellner-Rogers, 1996) calls "intelligent action." That involves using standards and engaging teachers in student-related professional development as a part of the "everydayness" of what they do. Then all youngsters will be assured that they have the opportunity to learn. This "intelligent action" begins with NSDC's Standards for Staff Development Revised. According to Shirley Hord (Roy & Hord, 2003) of the Southwest Educational Development Laboratory (SEDL) in the Introduction to *Moving NSDC's Staff Development Standards into Practice: Innovation Configurations,* the standards are "informative and provocative, but not regulatory. They are clear and direct." This easy-to-understand document on staff development standards expedites the planning for William's district and should be a linchpin for program planning in all districts.

The NSDC standards are directly applicable to the PLP, either in the planning or in the implementation phases, or both. The three domains in the standards include context, process, and content. These standards may be viewed at www.nsdc.org. The design team in William's district joined together in a study group to examine the standards carefully. That led them to the completion of the planning model for the PLP that was previously shown in Figure 2.7. To assist in the development process, the members of the study group systematically analyzed the following questions:

- What do students need teachers to do so teachers have a deep understanding of reading?
- What do students need teachers to do so teachers can carry out deliberate instruction in reading, spelling, and writing?
- What do students need teachers to do so that they learn how to explicitly teach students the skills they themselves are learning?
- What do students need teachers to do so teachers can reinforce their learning about critical attributes of the new practice?

You will note that the questions are presented in a unique format, but they are specifically written that way to reinforce the fact that the professional development design will be about the desired learning for students. The questioning model itself is adapted from the model presented by Carlene Murphy and Mike Murphy in Easton's (2004) book *Powerful Designs for Professional Learning.*

THE PLP AND THE PROFESSIONAL GROWTH DESIGN

The team focused on various designs for professional growth using *Powerful Designs for Professional Learning* (Easton, 2004) and selected those designs that would help the group meet the local goal of the PLP. More than one design was selected, because the PLP will be more productive if it has a staff development component built around a strategic plan that joins several models together. Guskey (2000) gives additional reasons for combining staff development models. If they are linked in thoughtful ways, the combined models can (1) provide a highly effective means of improvement at both the individual and the district level; and 2) help to ensure that the staff development efforts remain intentional, ongoing, and systemic. Therefore, during the four-week span of the PLP, several of the following models are incorporated into the design in order to improve student learning. The components, descriptions, and the attributes of each as used in the PLP include:

1. **A lab-based learning design.** Description: an organized structure that will provide support and opportunities for growth to the teachers, coaches, and administrators to help them reach the program's goal. Included in the implementation of the concept is the establishment of a collaborative culture; time set aside for learning; discussion, dialogue, and analyzing data; personalized feedback; and a focus on subject matter. Teachers will implement their new learning from the afternoon sessions during the morning clinics with a 1:6, or smaller, student-teacher ratio.

2. **A collaborative culture.** Description: three or four educators working together to discuss student work with a "critical friend's eye" (Bella, 2004) and discussing their role in what is taught (curriculum), how they affected what is taught (instruction), and how to measure what is taught and learned (assessment). Judith Warren Little (1990) calls a collaborative culture "our most effective tool for improving instruction." Even though the PLP is an awareness-level program for students, by reviewing students' work and discussing it according to current research and practice, teachers will be better prepared to understand and appreciate students of varying abilities and instruction at different levels of mastery.

3. **Subject-specific training.** Description: an essential staff development ingredient because "the most powerful form of staff development occurs at the intersection of content and pedagogy" (Lee Shulman as told to Dennis Sparks, 1992). By focusing on the subject-specific need (in this program the need is reading) of the students in the achievement gap, the teachers can increase their understanding of the problems, topics, issues, and elements that constitute the subject's curriculum. Subject-specific staff development is likely to be more rich and textured than generic staff development.

4. **Coaching with feedback.** Description: a staff development element used in the PLP to provide respectful, collegial reflection about instructional decisions (Harwell-Kee, 1999) and provide a process that will accelerate successful skill development. Through feedback, teachers will frame the purpose of their work, understand its importance, and be

enabled to improve their practice through self-assessment and self-adjustment.

5. **Reflection**. Description: a staff development element that includes "an active thought process aimed at understanding and subsequent improvement" (York-Barr, Sommers, Ghere, & Montie, 2001). In the PLP, reflection will occur both formally and informally. The goal of the reflection is to provide an avenue for teachers to gain a deeper understanding and insight into their teaching of reading so that they can make a difference in the lives of students. They can achieve this goal by actively and consciously processing their thoughts about their instructional practices in reading.

6. **Study groups**. Description: a staff development element that has "a small group of teachers joining together to increase their capacities through new learning for the benefit of students" (Murphy & Lick, 1998). In the PLP, this process helped the design team to collaboratively acquire and develop the knowledge and skills necessary to develop all facets of the program.

7. **Educator journaling**. Description: visual thinking in written form. In the PLP, journaling will help teachers clarify their understanding of teaching reading, give insight into their teaching practices, help them sort out connections between theory and practice, and give them a safe place to generate new hypotheses for action (Taggart & Wilson, 1998).

8. **Previewing instruction**. Description: model teaching of an element of the next day's lesson to familiarize teachers with the design qualities that are included in each lesson. This type of instruction will help teachers make connections by visualizing what will happen when they teach the lesson themselves. It also helps in understanding and alignment of the instruction to the genre of the curriculum.

9. **Analyzing lessons**. Description: a staff development element that keeps the teacher true to the acquisition lesson design (Bella, 2004). Teachers in the PLP can be flexible during the instructional time in order to meet the needs of students or capture a teachable moment, but the design characteristics of the acquisition lesson that have been embedded in the lesson should remain in place and be the basis of discussions around the what, why, and how of delivery.

10. **Classroom walk-throughs.** Definition: a staff development process used by administrators in the PLP to keep the classes focused on teaching and learning. The principal notes the curriculum presentation and the instructional strategies that are being employed. That information is then used to structure dialogue with teachers about pedagogical approaches used in the PLP, which may be used in the teacher's classroom during the regular school year. Thus, this element becomes a bridge to tomorrow.

11. **Measurement and review procedures.** Definition: analyzing and reviewing how data are used in the PLP. This staff development component informs structural decisions and supports the development of new strategies to improve student learning.

12. **Training for skill development**. Definition: an efficient staff development process for sharing a knowledge base and developing a common vocabulary. The training sessions in the PLP are highly organized, and have clearly articulated teacher outcomes and explicit expectations. All the sessions are supplemented with follow-up activities and provide the feedback and coaching necessary for successful improvement.

THE ROLE OF THE ADMINISTRATOR AND COACH

Garmston and Wellman (1997) explain the need for a dynamic system for developing professional capacities. Among the six major areas of knowledge that they say are necessary, this is one that focuses on *the ability to have collegial interaction.* Three groups of educators are involved in the day-to-day implementation of the PLP: teachers, coaches, and administrators. Individuals within the groups were selected in William's district (see Chapter 3) based on an application process for their role, by analyzing the way they exhibited the knowledge, skills, and attitudes that are present in effective educators. Educators share the major values of the district and, according to their written applications, their professional learning needs are likely to be met by working in the program. All teachers, coaches, and administrators will thus use their own unique skills to form productive work teams at the building level—talking together, thinking insightfully together about critical issues, and acting together in ways that are creative and coordinated.

Each group has role definitions to assist them as they work. See Figure 6.1 for role descriptions for the principal and the feedback coach.

On a more specific note, the questions that a feedback coach might use in a dialogue with teachers in the program are shown in Figure 6.2, and questions that principals may ask teachers are in Figure 6.3.

LAB-BASED STAFF DEVELOPMENT

"The research is abundantly clear: Nothing motivates a child more than when learning is valued by schools, families, and communities working together in partnership. . . . These forms of involvement do not happen by action or even invitation. They happen by explicit strategic intervention." These words by Michael Fullan (2004) set the stage for telling you about the centerpiece of the PLP, the lab-based staff development program. In order to send a clear signal to the participants of the importance of the goals and actions of the program, the ITF developed and implemented an intensive 22-day learning experience in which to immerse all the educators who were involved. Two preparatory days

Figure 6.1 The Principal's Role Defined

- Advocate for and facilitate collaborative interaction among staff with expected outcomes identified.
- Provide classroom coaching experiences to assist with the implementation of the curriculum and instructional design of the PLP.
- Work with staff to clearly describe classroom practices and communicate expectations for implementation.
- Conduct classroom walk-throughs to gain information to encourage teacher reflection.
- Communicate a strong vision for program to staff and community.
- Clearly define and uphold expectations for staff and student learning.
- Participate, along with teachers, in all educator lab sessions, as a leader, facilitator, or participant.
- Serve as a role model in how to address conflicts productively.
- Accept no excuses for the lack of achievement by the students in the achievement gap.
- Model respectful dialogue among staff regarding the role in helping all students learn.
- Assist teachers in developing activities that promote student learning.

- Keep the cumulative records for the program and ensure that they are returned to the base school.
- Ensure that multiple data sources—as required by the program design—are collected and reported to the appropriate evaluator.
- Conduct both formative and summative evaluation of all components of the program.
- Know that the most powerful professional development is "part of the work of daily teaching" and "is seamless with teaching" (Sparks, 2005).

Figure 6.2 Feedback: Coaches' Conversation Starters

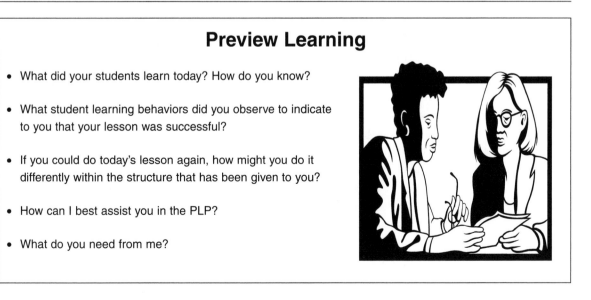

Preview Learning

- What did your students learn today? How do you know?
- What student learning behaviors did you observe to indicate to you that your lesson was successful?
- If you could do today's lesson again, how might you do it differently within the structure that has been given to you?
- How can I best assist you in the PLP?
- What do you need from me?

Figure 6.3   The Principals' Questions for Teachers

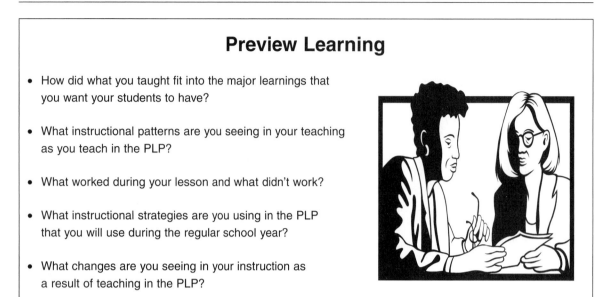

Preview Learning

- How did what you taught fit into the major learnings that you want your students to have?

- What instructional patterns are you seeing in your teaching as you teach in the PLP?

- What worked during your lesson and what didn't work?

- What instructional strategies are you using in the PLP that you will use during the regular school year?

- What changes are you seeing in your instruction as a result of teaching in the PLP?

preceded the actual 20-day Preview Learning Program where the teachers and students learned on the job together.

STAFF DEVELOPMENT AGENDAS

Comprehensive agendas for each of the 22 days follow. They may be used as a model for developing strategic intervention actions, activities, and events that will maximize learning opportunities for students and, at the same time, enhance the professional learning of teachers. The agendas will bring clarity to each professional role. Figure 6.4 provides the detail for the preparatory sessions followed by the extensive blueprint for the 20-day exemplary professional learning and growth opportunity in Figure 6.5.

When you read the entire agenda for the 20 days of staff development, you will find that high levels of commitment are required from teachers, coaches, and administrators, and even for the external and internal consultants who train for skill development. The schedule displays a significant change from the way staff development usually occurs with teachers, but it supports a well-conceived, multiple-strategy program model that requires intellectual energy from all participants. That is one of the reasons that the task force in William's district used a structured teacher selection process (see Chapter 3).

The 20-day agenda focuses on teaching participants how to do what is required to develop successful readers in students and thoughtful learners in adults. This is accomplished through some of the following.

- Individual reflection and collaboration with others are a given. The design encourages educators to talk openly about their teaching and use a common language.

Figure 6.4   Preview Learning Agenda, Days One and Two: "Getting Ready"

8:00-8:30	Registration. Collect resources (Agendas; Grade-level curriculum; Teaching resources; Bios on trainers; Staff roster; Room assignments; Student data)
8:45-9:30	Welcome and Icebreaker. Talk to three people that you do not know. Move from one to the other when the bell is sounded. Tell:

- Your name
- Your base school and grade you teach
- Your PLP school and grade you will teach
- One thing you would like this person to know about you

8:45-9:30	Overview of the Design of the PLP.

- What it is
- What it isn't
- Why you are here; your role and responsibility in this program
- Student population
- Meet the administrators, coaches, internal trainers (teacher leaders)
- The role of the administrator in the PLP
- The role of the coach in the PLP
- The role of the internal trainer in the PLP
- The role of the external trainer in the PLP

9:30-9:45	Break
9:45-10:30	Overview of the Four-Week Agenda, Curriculum, Instruction, and Schedules
10:30-11:30	"Introduction to Assessment: "Assessment of Learning and Assessment for Learning: The What, When, Why, and How" (External Consultant)
11:30-12:00	Lunch (catered in)
12:00-1:30	"Assessment," continued.
1:30-1:45	Break
1:45-3:15	"Assessment," continued.
3:15-3:30	Comment Cards. Pluses for the day. A question you may have at this point.

Preview Learning Agenda: Day Two "Getting Ready"

8:00-8:15	Welcome and Icebreaker. Talk to two people you do not know. Move from one to the other when the bell is sounded. Tell:

- Your name
- Your base school and grade you teach
- Your PLP school and grade you will teach
- Your best hopes for the PLP

8:15-8:30	Respond to Comment Cards
8:30-9:30	"Professional Learning" (PLP Facilitator)

- What it is
- What it isn't
- Why you are here
- Your role and responsibility for professional growth

(Continued)

Figure 6.4 (Continued)

9:30-9:45	Break
9:45-11:30	"Powerful Designs for Professional Learning" (Resource: Easton, 2004)
11:30-12:00	Lunch (catered in)
12:00-1:30	"What Effective Teachers of Reading Should Know and Be Able to Do" (Internal Consultant, PLP Facilitator)
1:30-1:45	Break
1:45-3:15	"Effective Teachers of Reading," continued.
3:15-3:30	Comment Cards. Pluses for the day. A question you may have at this point.

See you in July!!!

- Modeling, for teachers, strategies that will be used with students prepares the educators in advance for their leadership role.
- Teachers at the same grade level have the opportunity to work together academically, instructionally, and behaviorally.
- Grade-level curriculum content and instructional processes are scaffolded in the learning process for educators, and removed systematically to aid in translating the instruction into effective practice.
- Guiding questions, suggestions for follow-up staff development for each component, and expected outcomes promote conscious and reflective thinking about the norms as the days unfold.
- The agenda focuses on knowledge. E. D. Hirsch, Jr. (1989), says this will narrow the gap that exists in the target population.

The National Staff Development Council promotes job-embedded staff development for educators as part of their daily work. The teacher who operates at an awareness level of options for job-embedded professional learning, however, often questions how he can interact with students, guide their instruction, and tend to his professional learning at the same time. Optional job-embedded activities used in the PLP serve as a guide for all teachers, regardless of their assignments, and are offered here as examples in Figure 6.6. In the PLP, teachers embedded these activities as appropriate in their morning time with students.

SCHEDULING

The schedule that was used in the PLP in William's district during the morning for teachers, coaches, and administrators may be reviewed by looking at the master schedule shown in Figure 6.7. All groups of educators were expected to participate fully in all the afternoon sessions shown in Figure 6.5, as well as the preparatory meetings exhibited in Figure 6.4.

(*Text continues on page 129*)

Figure 6.5: Preview Learning
Staff Development Agenda for Teachers, Coaches, and Administrators
12:00 – 4:00
Week One, Monday

Site Code: 1 = Individual School
2 = Staff Development Center
3 = Individual Option

Time	Staff Development Design	Topic	Site	Leader or Facilitator	Guiding Question	Follow-up Staff Development	Expected Outcome(s)	Notes
12:30-12:40	Collaborative Culture	Icebreaker: E-Talk. Meet and greet four different people who teach in sites different from your site. "My name is ____. Here is my email address to 'talk' about the progress our students are making. I am happy to be here because ____."	2	PLP Facilitator (Put conversation on overhead transparency)	What can get the educators to interact with each other?	Journaling	• Contribute to a collaborative culture	• Write name & email on four different index cards • Time • Blow whistle for signal to move
12:40-2:00	Reflection Training for Skill Development	Reflection & Reflective Practice: (Part I) • What is reflection and reflective practice? • Collaborative Culture: Purpose and norms • Application	2	Consultant A (External)	In reflecting on my students and instruction today, what action on my part will most likely influence my student's capacity to read better?	Educator Journaling	Time invested in reflecting will: • bring greater student learning • enhance feelings of efficacy in teachers • bring a more collaborative culture to the program	• Consultant to monitor reflection sessions remainder of day to determine emerging needs for tomorrow
2:00-2:15		Break						• Reconvene in grade-level groups
2:15-3:00	Previewing Instruction	**Teaching for Tomorrow** • Model teach tomorrow's lesson for Word Study Strand • Introduce the skills and concepts presented in tomorrow's Guided Reading Strand, Skills and Language Strand, and Writing Strand.	2	Coaches	How can I as a teacher use this preview lesson to make meaningful connections to the instructing that I will do tomorrow?	• Lab-based staff development • Coaching with feedback • Reflection	• Ability to teach skills explicitly and directly • Application of effective instructional strategies to teach reading	• Grade-level groups • Discuss curriculum and instruction alignment across the strands • Teachers take notes as required • Follow along with written lesson plan • Reconvene in large group

95

Figure 6.5: Preview Learning

Staff Development Agenda for Teachers, Coaches, and Administrators
12:00 – 4:00
Week One, Monday
(Continued)

Site Code: 1 = Individual School
2 = Staff Development Center
3 = Individual Option

Time	Staff Development Design	Topic	Site	Leader or Facilitator	Guiding Question	Follow-up Staff Development	Expected Outcome(s)	Notes
3:00-3:05		Travel Break	2					Reconvene in site-specific groups
3:05-3:55	Reflection Coaching With Feedback	**Rotation Block:** (a) Independent, silent reflection and review of observation of model teaching. Write follow-up questions in ThinkBook. Ask during individual dialogue with coach. (b) Coach holds up to three twenty-minute sessions for collegial reflection about instructional behaviors and decisions. (c) Administrators join in dialogue about lessons, their strengths and weaknesses, and student response to active participation in lessons.	2	(a) Individual (b) Coach (c) Administrator	How can I replace hunches with facts concerning my strengths? How can I expand my growth edge?	• Reflection • Lesson analysis • Journaling	• Ability to reflect independently on instructional effectiveness • Ability to engage in a provocative discussion with others about student learning	• Rotate from (a) to (b) to (c) with coach determining the rotation schedule for each individual teacher
3:55-4:00	Evaluation	Comment Cards	2	PLP Facilitator	What is one thing that I have learned today that will affect my learning in a positive way?			• Coaches collect and review for emerging needs

Figure 6.5: Preview Learning
Staff Development Agenda for Teachers, Coaches, and Administrators
12:00 – 4:00
Week One, Tuesday

Site Code: 1 = Individual School
2 = Staff Development Center
3 = Individual Option

Time	Staff Development Design	Topic	Site	Leader or Facilitator	Guiding Question	Follow-up Staff Development	Expected Outcome(s)	Notes
12:30-12:40	Collaborative Culture Analyzing Lessons	Reflective Icebreaker: Partners in turn – Identify a specific learning episode that happened with a student this morning. Tell how it related to your instruction	2	PLP Facilitator	How can I connect my teaching to increased learning for students?	Journaling	• Reflective teaching	• Dyads • Five minutes per person • Select partner from another school site and remain partners for three consecutive sessions.
12:40-2:00	Reflection Training for Skill Development	Reflection & Reflective Practice (Part II): • Ways of Talking • Which One When • Application	2	Consultant A (External)	What data will best inform my practice as I teach students in the PLP?	• Journaling • Reflection with a partner	• Ability to verbally share & think together for the purpose of making connections, increasing understanding, and generating possibilities (York-Barr et al., 2001)	
2:00-2:15		Break						• Reconvene in grade-level groups
2:15-3:00	Previewing Instruction	**Teaching for Tomorrow** • Model teach tomorrow's lesson for Guided Reading Strand • Introduce the skills and concepts presented in tomorrow's Word Study Strand, Skills and Language Strand, and Writing Strand.	2	Coaches	How can I as a teacher use this preview lesson to make meaningful connections to the instructing that I will do tomorrow?	• Lab-based instruction with students • Coaching with feedback • Reflection	• Application of effective instructional strategies to teach reading • Ability to instruct strategically • Ability to teach skills explicitly and directly	• Grade-level groups • Discuss curriculum and instruction alignment across the strands • Teachers take notes as required • Follow along with written lesson plan

Figure 6.5: Preview Learning

Staff Development Agenda for Teachers, Coaches, and Administrators

12:00 – 4:00

Week One, Tuesday

(Continued)

Site Code: 1 = Individual School
2 = Staff Development Center
3 = Individual Option

Time	Staff Development Design	Topic	Site	Leader or Facilitator	Guiding Question	Follow-up Staff Development	Expected Outcome(s)	Notes
3:00-3:05		Travel Break	2	(a) Individual (b) Coach (c) Administrator				• Convene in site-specific groups
3:05-3:55	Reflection Coaching With Feedback	**Rotation Block:** (a) Independent, silent reflection and review of observation of model teaching. Write follow-up questions in Think Book. Discuss with coach. (b) Coach holds up to three twenty-minute sessions for collegial reflection about instructional behaviors and decisions (c) Administrators have dialogue 1:1 about classroom walk-through	2		How will reflective thinking help me have a higher-level thinking process? How will my higher-order level thinking process effect an increase in student learning?	• Reflection • Coaching • Journaling	• Ability to reflect independently on instructional effectiveness • Ability to engage in a provocative discussion with others about student learning	• Rotate from (a) to (b) to (c) with the coach determining the rotation schedule for each individual teacher
3:55-4:00	Evaluation	Comment Cards	2	Administrator	What is one thing that I learned today that will affect student learning in a positive way?			• Coaches collect and review for emerging needs

Figure 6.5: Preview Learning
Staff Development Agenda for Teachers, Coaches, and Administrators
12:00 – 4:00
Week One, Wednesday

Site Code: 1 = Individual School
2 = Staff Development Center
3 = Individual Option

Time	Staff Development Design	Topic	Site	Leader or Facilitator	Guiding Question	Follow-up Staff Development	Expected Outcome(s)	Notes
12:30-12:40	Collaborative Culture Analyzing Lessons	Reflective Icebreaker: Partners in turn. Use the same event from yesterday, but put yourself in the student's place. Talk about your instruction from the viewpoint of a student.	2	PLP Facilitator	How can I connect my teaching to increased learning for students?	Journaling	• Reflective teaching	• Dyads • Five minutes per person • Continue with yesterday's partner
12:40-2:00	Reflection Training for Skill Development	Reflection and Reflective Practice (Part III) • Structure for on-going reflection • Application	2	Consultant A (External)	How can I use the knowledge and skills of my colleagues to become a more effective teacher?	Interactive journaling	• On-going dialogue that occurs outside the face-to-face meetings	• Interactive part of journaling will occur every two weeks when teachers exchange journals and make inquiries in writing to expand thinking
2:00-2:15		Break						• Reconvene in grade-level groups
2:15-3:00	Previewing Instruction	**Teaching for Tomorrow** • Model teach tomorrow's lesson for Skills and Language Strand • Introduce the skills and concepts presented in tomorrow's Word Study Strand, Guided Reading Strand, and Writing Strand.	2	Coaches	How can I, as a teacher, use this preview lesson to make meaningful connections to the instructing that I will do tomorrow?	• Lab-based instruction with students • Coaching with feedback • Reflection	• Application of effective instructional strategies to teach reading • Ability to instruct strategically • Ability to teach skills explicitly and directly	• Grade-level groups • Discuss curriculum and instruction alignment across the strands • Teachers take notes as required • Follow along with written lesson plan

Staff Development Agenda for Teachers, Coaches, and Administrators
12:00 – 4:00
Week One, Wednesday
(Continued)

Site Code:	1 = Individual School
	2 = Staff Development Center
	3 = Individual Option

Time	Staff Development Design	Topic	Site	Leader or Facilitator	Guiding Question	Follow-up Staff Development	Expected Outcome(s)	Notes
3:00-3:05		Travel Break	2					• Convene in site-specific groups
3:05-3:55	Reflection Coaching with Feedback	**Rotation Block** (a) Independent reflection and review of observation of model teaching. Write follow-up questions in Think Book. Ask during individual dialogue with coach. (b) Coach holds up to three twenty-minute sessions for collegial reflection about instructional behaviors and decisions. (c) Administrators have dialogue about classroom walk-through.	2	(a) Individual (b) Coach (c) Administrator	How will reflective thinking help me have a higher-level thinking process? How will my higher-level thinking process effect an increase in student learning?	• Reflection • Lesson analysis • Journaling	• Ability to reflect independently on instructional effectiveness • Ability to engage in a provocative discussion with others about student learning	• Rotate from (a) to (b) to (c) with the coach determining the rotation schedule for each individual teacher
3:55-4:00	Evaluation	Comment Cards	2	Administrator	What is one thing that I learned today that will affect student learning in a positive way?			• Coaches collect and review for emerging needs

Figure 6.5: Preview Learning
Staff Development Agenda for Teachers, Coaches, and Administrators
12:00 – 4:00
Week One, Thursday

Site Code: 1 = Individual School
2 = Staff Development Center
3 = Individual Option

Time	Staff Development Design	Topic	Site	Leader or Facilitator	Guiding Question	Follow-up Staff Development	Expected Outcome(s)	Notes
12:30-12:40	Collaborative Culture Analyzing lessons	Reflective Icebreaker: Partners in turn – Use the same event or experience from yesterday. Explain how someone on a balcony, being an unseen observer, might look down on and interpret the event or experience.	2	PLP Facilitator	How can I connect my teaching to increased student learning?	• Journaling	• Reflective teaching	• Dyads • Five minutes per person • Continue with yesterday's partner
12:40-2:00	Collaborative Culture Training for Skill Development	Looking at Student Work (Part I) • A Tuning Protocol: Critical Elements; Steps • Application	2	PLP Facilitator as Moderator & Consultant B (Internal: Panel of teachers in district that are skilled in the process of looking at student work)	How can I present students' work to a group of thoughtful educators for a structured conversation aimed at "tuning" the work to higher standards?	• Individual and group questioning: What can I do next to help the student learn?	• Ability to calibrate the quality of learning	• Teachers bring a sample of student work
2:00-2:15		Break	2					• Reconvene in grade-level groups
2:15-3:00	Previewing Instruction	**Teaching for Tomorrow** • Model teach tomorrow's lesson for the Writing Strand • Introduce the skills and concepts presented in tomorrow's Word Study Strand, Guided Reading Strand, and Skills and Language Strand	2	Coaches	How can I, as a teacher, use this preview lesson to make meaningful connections to the instruction that I will do tomorrow?	• Lab-based instruction with students • Coaching with feedback • Reflection	• Application of effective instructional strategies to teach reading • Ability to instruct strategically • Ability to teach skills explicitly and directly	• Grade-level groups • Discuss curriculum and instruction alignment across the strands • Teachers take notes as required • Follow along on written lesson plan

Figure 6.5: Preview Learning

Staff Development Agenda for Teachers, Coaches, and Administrators

12:00 – 4:00

Week One, Thursday

(Continued)

Site Code: 1 = Individual School
2 = Staff Development Center
3 = Individual Option

Time	Staff Development Design	Topic	Site	Leader or Facilitator	Guiding Question	Follow-up Staff Development	Expected Outcome(s)	Notes
3:00-3:05		Travel Break	2					• Convene in site-specific groups
3:05-3:55	Reflection Coaching with Feedback	**Rotation Block** (a) Independent reflection and review of observation of model teaching. Write follow-up questions and thoughts in Think Book to share with coach. (b) Coach holds up to three twenty-minute sessions for collegial reflection about instructional behaviors and decisions (c) Administrators have 1:1 dialogue about classroom walk-through	2	(a) Individual (b) Coach (c) Administrator	How will reflective thinking help me have a higher-level thinking process? How will my higher-level thinking process effect an increase in student learning?	• Reflection • Lesson analysis • Journaling	• Ability to reflect independently on instructional effectiveness • Ability to engage in a provocative discussion with others about student learning	• Rotate from (a) to (b) to (c) with each coach determining the rotation schedule for each individual teacher
3:55-4:00	Evaluation	Comment Cards	2	Administrator	What is one thing that I learned today that will affect student learning in a positive way?			• Coaches collect and review for emerging needs

Figure 6.5: Preview Learning

Staff Development Agenda for Teachers, Coaches, and Administrators

12:00 – 4:00

Week One, Friday

Site Code: 1 = Individual School
2 = Staff Development Center
3 = Individual Option

Time	Staff Development Design	Topic	Site	Leader or Facilitator	Guiding Question	Follow-up Staff Development	Expected Outcome(s)	Notes
12:30-12:45	Journaling Reflection	Write in the Think Book: "How I connected my instruction to increased student learning during the first four days of this week."	1	School Administrator	How can I connect my teaching to increased learning for students?	• Coaching	• Reflective practice	• Individuals independently writing within the large group setting
12:45-1:00	Collaborative Discussion	Processing and Application: Share concepts that have emerged through the four days of reflective icebreakers.	1	School Administrator with coach charting ideas			• Collaborative culture	• Coach charts ideas • Teachers take notes as required
1:00-3:30	Analyzing Lessons Reviewing Student Work	Looking at Student Work: Review Student Progress to Date • Analyze student responses to questions (see Chapter 7) to discuss strengths and weaknesses of instructional periods as perceived by students • Determine class patterns of improvement	1	School Administrator and Coach	What specific new skills have my students achieved this week? How can I link those improved skills to my teaching?	• Collaborative planning	• Connections between effective teaching and student learning	• Group by grade-levels or in primary and intermediate groups if a small faculty • Coaches participate as required using questioning techniques • Select group recorder • Turn in group notes at SD Center on Monday • Bring students' portfolios
3:30-4:00	Reflection	**Journal Writing** Complete the sentence stem: "My thoughts, in synthesized form, to the week's Guiding Questions, include _____."	1	Coach (Review Guiding Questions for the week)	What understandings and information do I have that I can use to target a more effective practice in teaching reading?	• Interactive journaling	• Collaboration	• Exchange synthesized response with a colleague who will respond and make inquiries back to you in writing. Return comments due Tuesday

103

Figure 6.5: Preview Learning
Staff Development Agenda for Teachers, Coaches, and Administrators
12:00 – 4:00
Week Two, Monday

Site Code: 1 = Individual School
2 = Staff Development Center
3 = Individual Option

Time	Staff Development Design	Topic	Site	Leader or Facilitator	Guiding Question	Follow-up Staff Development	Expected Outcome(s)	Notes
12:30-12:40	Collaborative Culture, Analyzing Lessons	Reflective Icebreaker: Partners in turn – Complete the sentence, "Three ways that my teaching this morning was like planting a garden are_____ ."	2	PLP Facilitator	How can I connect my teaching to increased student learning?	• Journaling	• Reflective teaching	• Dyads • A new partner from a different school to be partner for the week • Stand and talk • Five minutes per person • Coaches collect notes from Friday's discussion
12:40-2:00	Collaborative Culture, Training for Skill Development	Looking at Student Work (Part II) Checklists Rubrics, Rigor, and Results Designing a Rubric Terminology Application	2	PLP Facilitator as Moderator and Consultant B (Internal panel of teachers from the district that are skilled in the process of looking at student work)	How can I present students' work to a group of thoughtful educators for a structured conversation aimed at clarity in student expectations?	• Individual and group questioning: What can I do next to help this student learn? • In-class observation followed by feedback coaching	• Ability to calibrate the quality of learning	• Teachers bring a sample of student work
2:00-2:15		Break	2					• Reconvene in grade-level groups
2:15-3:00	Previewing Instruction	**Teaching for Tomorrow** • Model teach tomorrow's lesson for Word Study Strand. • Introduce the skills and concepts presented in tomorrow's Guided Reading Strand, Skills and Language Strand, and Writing Strand	2	Coaches	How can I, as a teacher, use this preview lesson to make meaningful connections to the instructing that I will do tomorrow?	• Lab-based instruction with students • Coaching with feedback • Reflection	• Application of effective instructional strategies to teach reading • Ability to instruct strategically • Ability to teach skills explicitly and directly	• Grade-level group • Discuss curriculum and instruction alignment as it occurs across the strands • Follow along on written lesson plan

Figure 6.5: Preview Learning

Staff Development Agenda for Teachers, Coaches, and Administrators
12:00 – 4:00
Week Two, Monday
(Continued)

Site Code: 1 = Individual School
2 = Staff Development Center
3 = Individual Option

Time	Staff Development Design	Topic	Site	Leader or Facilitator	Guiding Question	Follow-up Staff Development	Expected Outcome(s)	Notes
3:00-3:05		Travel Break	2					• Convene in site-specific groups
3:05-3:55	Reflection Coaching with Feedback	**Rotation Block** (a) Independent reflection and review of model as presented. Write follow-up questions about the content and instructional strategies that were used in the model teaching in Think Books for follow-up discussion with the coach. (b) Coach holds up to three twenty-minute sessions of collegial reflection about instructional behaviors and decisions. (c) Administrators have dialogue about classroom walk-through.	2	(a) Individual (b) Coach (c) Administrator	How will reflective thinking help me have a higher-level thinking process? How will my higher-level thinking process effect an increase in student learning?	• Reflection • Coaching • Journaling	• Ability to reflect independently on instructional effectiveness • Ability to engage in a provocative discussion with others about student learning	• Rotate from (a) to (b) to (c) with the coach determining the rotation schedule for each individual teacher
3:55-4:00	Evaluation	Comment Cards	2	Administrator	How can I use what I learned today to affect student learning in a positive way?			• Coaches collect and review for emerging needs • Remind teachers that interactive journals are due back to the owner tomorrow

105

Figure 6.5: Preview Learning
Staff Development Agenda for Teachers, Coaches, and Administrators
12:00 – 4:00
Week Two, Tuesday

Site Code: 1 = Individual School
2 = Staff Development Center
3 = Individual Option

Time	Staff Development Design	Topic	Site	Leader or Facilitator	Guiding Question	Follow-up Staff Development	Expected Outcome(s)	Notes
12:30-12:40	Collaborative Culture. Analyzing Lessons	Reflective Icebreaker: Partners in turn – Complete the sentence: "Three ways that my teaching this morning was like being at the beach include _____."	2	PLP Facilitator	How can I connect my teaching to increased learning for students?	• Journaling	• Reflective teaching	• Coach: request interactive journal partners to return journals to owners • Week two partner • Stand and talk • Five minutes per person
12:40-2:00	Training for Skill Development	Using Guided Reading to Improve Reading (Part I)	2	Consultant C (External: A reading specialist in guided reading)	How can I empower students with independent reading skills and strategies that they can use to interpret texts and other reading material?	• Journaling • Lab-based instruction with students • Feedback coaching	• How to guide instruction that coordinates to students' needs • Ability to provide a scaffold of support to students with learning difficulties in the area of reading	
2:00-2:15		Break						
2:15-3:00	Previewing Instruction	**Teaching for Tomorrow** • Model teach tomorrow's lesson for Guided Reading Strand • Introduce the skills and concepts presented in tomorrow's Word Study Strand, Skills and Language Strand, and Writing Strand	2	Coaches	How can I, as a teacher, use this preview lesson to make meaningful connections to the instructing that I will do tomorrow?	• Lab-based instruction with students • Coaching with feedback • Reflection	• Application of effective instructional strategies to teach reading • Ability to instruct strategically • Ability to teach skills explicitly and directly	• Reconvene in grade-level groups • Grade-level groups • Discuss curriculum and instruction alignment across the strands • Teachers take notes as required • Follow along on written lesson plans

Figure 6.5: Preview Learning
Staff Development Agenda for Teachers, Coaches, and Administrators
12:00 - 4:00
Week Two, Tuesday
(Continued)

Site Code: 1 = Individual School
2 = Staff Development Center
3 = Individual Option

Time	Staff Development Design	Topic	Site	Leader or Facilitator	Guiding Question	Follow-up Staff Development	Expected Outcome(s)	Notes
3:00-3:05		Travel Break	2					• Convene in site-specific groups
3:05-3:55	Reflection Coaching with Feedback	**Rotation Block** (a) Independent reflection and review of model as presented. Write follow-up questions about the content and instructional strategies that were used in the Model Teaching in Think Books for follow-up discussion with the coach. (b) Coach holds up to three twenty-minute sessions of collegial reflection about instructional behaviors and decisions. (c) Administrators have dialogue about classroom walk-through.	2	(a) Individual (b) Coach (c) Administrator	How will reflective thinking help me have a higher-level thinking process? How will my higher-level thinking process effect an increase in student learning?	• Reflection • Coaching • Journaling	• Ability to reflect independently on instructional effectiveness • Ability to engage in a provocative discussion with others about student learning	• Rotate from (a) to (b) to (c) with the coach determining the rotation schedule for each individual teacher
3:55-4:00	Evaluation	Comment Cards	2	Administrator	How can I use what I learned today to affect student learning in a positive way?			• Coaches collect and review for emerging needs

Figure 6.5: Preview Learning

Staff Development Agenda for Teachers, Coaches, and Administrators
12:00 – 4:00
Week Two, Wednesday

Site Code: 1 = Individual School
2 = Staff Development Center
3 = Individual Option

Time	Staff Development Design	Topic	Site	Leader or Facilitator	Guiding Question	Follow-up Staff Development	Expected Outcome(s)	Notes
12:30–12:40	Collaborative Culture Analyzing Lessons	Reflective Icebreaker: Partners in turn – Complete the sentence: "Three ways that my teaching this morning was like a brisk walk in the mountains are _____."	2	PLP Facilitator	How can I connect my teaching to increased learning for students?	• Journaling	• Reflective teaching	• Week two partner • Stand and talk • Five minutes per person
12:40–2:00	Training for Skill Development	Using Guided Reading to Improve Reading (Part II)	2	Consultant C (External: A reading specialist in guided reading)	How can I empower students with independent reading skills and strategies that they can use to interpret texts and other reading material?	• Journaling • Lab-based instruction with students • Feedback coaching	• How to guide instruction that coordinates to students' needs • Ability to provide a scaffold of support to students with learning difficulties in the area of reading	
2:00–2:15	Break							• Reconvene in grade-level groups
2:15–3:00	Previewing Instruction	**Teaching for Tomorrow** • Model teach tomorrow's lesson for Skills and Language Strand • Introduce the skills and concepts presented in tomorrow's Word Study Strand, Guided Reading Strand, and Writing Strand.	2	Coaches	How can I, as a teacher, use this preview lesson to make meaningful connections to the instructing that I will do tomorrow?	• Lab-based instruction with students • Coaching with feedback • Reflection	• Application of effective instructional strategies to teach reading • Ability to instruct strategically • Ability to teach skills explicitly and directly	• Grade-level groups • Discuss curriculum and instruction alignment across the strands • Teachers take notes as required • Teachers follow along in the script as coaches model-teach the written lesson plan

Figure 6.5: Preview Learning
Staff Development Agenda for Teachers, Coaches, and Administrators
12:00 – 4:00
Week Two, Wednesday
(Continued)

Site Code: 1 = Individual School
2 = Staff Development Center
3 = Individual Option

Time	Staff Development Design	Topic	Site	Leader or Facilitator	Guiding Question	Follow-up Staff Development	Expected Outcome(s)	Notes
3:00-3:05		Travel Break	2					• Convene in site-specific groups
3:05-3:55	Reflection Coaching with Feedback	**Rotation Block** (a) Independent reflection and review of model as presented. Write follow-up questions about the content and instructional strategies that were used in the Model Teaching in Think Books for follow-up discussions with the coach. (b) Coach holds up to three twenty-minute sessions for collegial reflection about instructional behaviors and decisions. (c) Administrators have dialogue about classroom walk-through.	2	(a) Individual (b) Coach (c) Administrator	How will reflective thinking help me have a higher-level thinking process? How will my higher-level thinking process effect an increase in student learning?	• Reflection • Coaching • Journaling	• Ability to reflect independently on instructional effectiveness • Ability to engage in a provocative discussion with others about student learning	• Rotate from (a) to (b) to (c) with the coach determining the rotation schedule for each individual teacher
3:55-4:00	Evaluation	Comment Cards	2	Administrator	How can I use what I learned today to affect student learning in a positive way?			• Coaches collect and review for emerging needs

109

Figure 6.5: Preview Learning

Staff Development Agenda for Teachers, Coaches, and Administrators
12:00 – 4:00
Week Two, Thursday

Site Code: 1 = Individual School
2 = Staff Development Center
3 = Individual Option

Time	Staff Development Design	Topic	Site	Leader or Facilitator	Guiding Question	Follow-up Staff Development	Expected Outcome(s)	Notes
12:30–12:40	Collaborative Culture, Analyzing Lessons	Reflective Icebreaker: Partners in turn – Complete the sentence: "If the light fixtures in my classroom had eyes, ears, and/or feelings, today they would have seen that my teaching was _____"	2	PLP Facilitator	How can I connect my teaching to increased learning for students?	• Journaling	• Reflective teaching	• Week two partner • Stand and talk • Five minutes per person
12:40–2:00	Training for Skill Development	Using Guided Reading to Improve Reading (Part III)	2	Consultant C (External: A reading specialist in guided reading)	How can I empower students with independent reading skills and strategies that they can use to interpret texts and other reading material?	• Journaling • Lab-based instruction with students • Feedback coaching	• How to guide instruction that coordinates to students' needs • Ability to provide a scaffold of support to students with learning difficulties in the area of reading	
2:00–2:15		Break						Reconvene in grade-level groups
2:15–3:00	Previewing Instruction	**Teaching for Tomorrow** • Model teach tomorrow's lesson for the Writing Strand • Introduce the skills and concepts presented in tomorrow's Word Study Strand, Guided Reading Strand, and Skills and Language Strand	2	Coaches	How can I, as a teacher, use this preview lesson to make meaningful connections to the instructing that I will do tomorrow?	• Lab-based instruction with students • Coaching with feedback • Reflection	• Application of effective instructional strategies to teach reading • Ability to instruct strategically • Ability to teach skills explicitly and directly	• Grade-level groups • Discuss curriculum and instruction alignment across the strands • Teachers take notes as required • Teachers follow along in the script as coaches model-teach the written lesson plan

110

Figure 6.5: Preview Learning

Staff Development Agenda for Teachers, Coaches, and Administrators
12:00 – 4:00
Week Two, Thursday
(Continued)

Site Code: 1 = Individual School
2 = Staff Development Center
3 = Individual Option

Time	Staff Development Design	Topic	Site	Leader or Facilitator	Guiding Question	Follow-up Staff Development	Expected Outcome(s)	Notes
3:00-3:05		Travel Break	2					• Convene in site-specific groups
3:05-3:55	Reflection Coaching with Feedback	**Rotation Block** (a) Independent reflection and review of model as presented. Write follow-up questions about the content and instructional strategies that were used in the Model Teaching in Think Books for follow-up discussions with the coach. (b) Coach holds up to three twenty-minute sessions of collegial reflection about instructional behaviors and decisions. (c) Administrators have dialogue about classroom walk-through.	2	(a) Individual (b) Coach (c) Administrator	How will reflective thinking help me have a higher-level thinking process? How will my higher-level thinking process effect an increase in student learning?	• Reflection • Coaching • Journaling	• Ability to reflect independently on instructional effectiveness • Ability to engage in a provocative discussion with others about student learning	• Rotate from (a) to (b) to (c) with the coach determining the rotation schedule for each individual teacher
3:55-4:00	Evaluation	Comment Cards	2	Administrator	How can I use what I learned today to affect student learning in a positive way?			• Coaches collect and review for emerging needs

Figure 6.5: Preview Learning

Staff Development Agenda for Teachers, Coaches, and Administrators

12:00 – 4:00

Week Two, Friday

Site Code: 1=Individual School
2=Staff Development Center
3=Individual Option

Time	Staff Development Design	Topic	Site	Leader or Facilitator	Guiding Question	Follow-up Staff Development	Expected Outcome(s)	Notes
12:30-12:45	Journaling, Reflection	Write in the Think Book. Complete the sentence: "Three or four things that I added to my teaching repertoire as a result of the two weeks of being in the PLP include _____."	1	School Administrator	How can my learning facilitate an increase in learning for my students?	• Coaching	• Reflective practice	• Individuals independently writing within the large group setting
12:45-1:00	Collaborative Discussion	Share specific insights you got as you wrote in your journal.	1	School Administrator with coach charting ideas			• Collaborative culture	• Coach charts ideas • Teachers take notes as required
1:00-3:30	Analyzing Lessons, Reviewing Student Work	Looking at Student Work: Review Student Progress to Date • Analyze student portfolios using student responses to questions (see Chapter 7) to discuss strengths and weaknesses of instructional periods as perceived by students • Determine class patterns of improvement	1	School Administrator and Coach	What specific new skills have my students achieved this week? How can I link those improved skills to my teaching?	• Collaborative planning	• Connections between effective teaching and student learning	• Group by grade-levels or in primary and intermediate groups if a small faculty • Coaches participate as required using questioning techniques • Select group recorder • Turn in group notes at SD Center on Monday • Bring students' portfolios
3:30-4:00	Reflection	**Journal Writing** Complete the sentence stem: "My thoughts, in synthesized form, to the week's Guiding Questions, include _____."	1	Coach (Review Guiding Questions for the week)	What understandings and information do I have that I can use to target a more effective practice in teaching reading?	• Interactive journaling	• Collaboration	• Give interactive journal to journal partner who will make inquiries back to you in writing. Return comments due on Monday

Figure 6.5: Preview Learning
Staff Development Agenda for Teachers, Coaches, and Administrators
12:00 – 4:00
Week Three, Monday

Site Code: 1 = Individual School
2 = Staff Development Center
3 = Individual Option

Time	Staff Development Design	Topic	Site	Leader or Facilitator	Guiding Question	Follow-up Staff Development	Expected Outcome(s)	Notes
12:30-12:40	Collaborative Culture, Reflective Thinking	Reflective Icebreaker: Partners in turn. Complete the sentence: "The underlying belief that I have of _____ about teaching was made real to me last week through ____."	2	PLP Facilitator	How can I connect my beliefs and assumptions about teaching and learning to my effectiveness in teaching?	• Journaling	• Reflective teaching	• Return interactive journal to journal partner • Collect notes from Friday's session • New Week Three partner • Stand and talk • Five minutes per person
12:40-2:00	Training for Skill Development	Teaching Writing in the Content Area: Reading	2	Consultant D (Internal: A teacher from the district with expertise in the topic)	How can I deepen my students' understanding of content and help them connect subject matter to their lives?	• Lab-based instruction with students • Coaching with feedback	• Ability to integrate writing assignments into the reading program	
2:00-2:15		Break						• Reconvene in grade-level groups
2:15-3:30	Collaborative Culture, Previewing and Analyzing Instruction	**Teaching for Tomorrow:** • Model teach tomorrow's lesson for Word Study Strand. Begin by temporarily scaffolding out the essential question. Scaffold out essential questions on remaining three strands as the concepts and skills of the lesson are presented. See notes column at right.	2	Coaches	How do I scaffold my thinking to write generalizations at a more sophisticated level?	• Writing a lesson collaboratively in grade-level groups	• How to use "How" or "Why" (not "What") in writing an essential question • How to write content-specific essential questions	• Turn a generalization into an essential question, i.e., words can help us make a picture of unknown places in our own minds. How can words help us make a . . .?

Figure 6.5: Preview Learning

Staff Development Agenda for Teachers, Coaches, and Administrators

12:00 – 4:00

Week Three, Monday

(Continued)

Site Code: 1 = Individual School
2 = Staff Development Center
3 = Individual Option

Time	Staff Development Design	Topic	Site	Leader or Facilitator	Guiding Question	Follow-up Staff Development	Expected Outcome(s)	Notes
3:30-3:55	Reflection, Active Learning	**Journal Writing** • Make five generalizations about new learnings for you. • Convert the generalizations into essential questions	2	Administrator with Coaches available for assistance	How can I think conceptually to plan a questioning path?		• Illuminated conceptual thinking	
3:55-4:00	Evaluation	Comment Cards	2	Administrator	How can I use what I've learned today to affect student learning in a positive way?			• Coaches collect and review for coaching options

Figure 6.5: Preview Learning

Site Code: 1 = Individual School
2 = Staff Development Center
3 = Individual Option

Staff Development Agenda for Teachers, Coaches, and Administrators
12:00 – 4:00
Week Three, Tuesday

Time	Staff Development Design	Topic	Site	Leader or Facilitator	Guiding Question	Follow-up Staff Development	Expected Outcome(s)	Notes
12:30-12:40	Collaborative Culture, Reflective Thinking	Reflective Icebreaker: Partners in Turn – Complete the sentence: "The underlying belief that I have of ____ about my professional growth was made personally meaningful to me yesterday or today when ____."	2	PLP Facilitator	How can I connect my beliefs and assumptions about teaching and learning to my effectiveness in teaching?	• Journaling	• Reflective teaching	• Week three partner • Stand and talk • Five minutes per person
12:40-2:00	Training for Skill Development	Vocabulary Development and Reading Fluency	2	Consultant E (Internal: A teacher from the district with expertise in the subject)	How can I most effectively teach vocabulary to my students?	• Lab-based instruction with students • Coaching with feedback	• Ability to provide instruction that actively involves students in building vocabulary • Ability to help students master phoneme manipulation, phonics, and initial word recognition skills	
2:00-2:15		Break	2					
2:15-3:30	Collaborative Culture, Previewing Instruction, Training for Skill Development	**Teaching for Tomorrow:** • Model teach tomorrow's lesson for Guided Instruction Strand. Scaffold out the Summarizing and Essential Question Revisited. • Review concepts and skills to be taught in remaining three strands. • Application. See notes column at right.	2	Coaches	How can scaffolding help me make meaningful connections to the teaching that I do?	• Writing a lesson collaboratively	• Clarity about the lessons' summarizing component and (1) its connection to the essential question, and (2) who does the summarizing • Ability to write an acquisition lesson	• Reconvene in grade-level groups • Let collaborative groups of teachers develop suggestions for the section "Summarizing and Essential Question Revisited"

Figure 6.5: Preview Learning
Staff Development Agenda for Teachers, Coaches, and Administrators
12:00 – 4:00
Week Three, Tuesday
(Continued)

Site Code: 1 = Individual School
2 = Staff Development Center
3 = Individual Option

Time	Staff Development Design	Topic	Site	Leader or Facilitator	Guiding Question	Follow-up Staff Development	Expected Outcome(s)	Notes
3:30–3:55	Analysis for Improvement	**Grade-level Discussion:** Reflect on answers to Guiding Questions today. Record aha's in the Think Book, if desired.	2	Coaches	How is what we are doing in the PLP ensuring that students are becoming aware of strategies that they can use to help them in the area of reading?	• Feedback coaching	• Clarity about curriculum design	
3:55–4:00	Evaluation	Comment Card	2	Coaches	How is the structure of the PLP working for you?			• Coaches collect and review for coaching options

Figure 6.5: Preview Learning
Staff Development Agenda for Teachers, Coaches, and Administrators
12:00 – 4:00
Week Three, Wednesday

Site Code: 1 = Individual School
2 = Staff Development Center
3 = Individual Option

Time	Staff Development Design	Topic	Site	Leader or Facilitator	Guiding Question	Follow-up Staff Development	Expected Outcome(s)	Notes
12:30-12:40	Collaborative Culture, Reflective Thinking	Reflective Icebreaker: Partners in Turn – Complete the sentence: "The underlying belief that I have of ____ about learning was reinforced today when ____."	2	PLP Facilitator	How can I connect my beliefs and assumptions about teaching and learning to my effectiveness in teaching?	• Journaling	• Reflective teaching	• Week Three partner • Stand and talk • Five minutes per person
12:40-2:00	Training for Skill Development	A Balanced Literacy Approach: Applying Running Records in Reading (Part I)	2	Consultant F (External)	How can using running records to enhance reading skills in students move me to higher levels of learning?	• Completing a running record followed by coaching feedback	• Teaching intentionally and explicitly	
2:00-2:15		Break						• Reconvene in grade-level groups
2:15-3:30	Collaborative Culture, Reviewing Instruction, Training for Skill Development	**Teaching for Tomorrow** • Model teach tomorrow's lesson for Skills and Language Strand. Scaffold out the Activating Learning Section during modeling. Review concepts and skills to be taught in the remaining three strands • Application. See notes column at right.	2	Coaches	How can scaffolding help me make meaningful connections to the teaching that I do?	• Writing a lesson collaboratively	• Clarity about the activating learning component and how it prepares the brain to receive input • Ability to write an acquisition lesson	• Collaborative groups develop suggestions for the section on Activating Learning in the Skills & Language Strand.

117

Figure 6.5: Preview Learning
Staff Development Agenda for Teachers, Coaches, and Administrators
12:00 – 4:00
Week Three, Wednesday
(Continued)

Site Code: 1 = Individual School
2 = Staff Development Center
3 = Individual Option

Time	Staff Development Design	Topic	Site	Leader or Facilitator	Guiding Question	Follow-up Staff Development	Expected Outcome(s)	Notes
3:30-3:55	Reflection, Collaborative Culture	**Journal Writing:** Record three types of activating learning strategies that have been used in the PLP that you feel most comfortable using. Stand and talk. Share written ideas with at least two people.	2	Coaches	How does the cognitive strategy of activating prime our cognitive pumps (McEwan, 2004) and provide a learning benefit?	• Writing a lesson collaboratively	• Teaching that is reflective and intentional	
3:55-4:00	Evaluation	**Stand and Talk:** Week Three Partners: "One important thing I've learned today is _____ because it squares with my beliefs on _____."	2	Coaches	How can I connect my beliefs and assumptions about teaching and learning to my effectiveness in teaching?		• Reflective teaching	

Figure 6.5: Preview Learning
Staff Development Agenda for Teachers, Coaches, and Administrators
12:00 – 4:00
Week Three, Thursday

Site Code: 1 = Individual School
2 = Staff Development Center
3 = Individual Option

Time	Staff Development Design	Topic	Site	Leader or Facilitator	Guiding Question	Follow-up Staff Development	Expected Outcome(s)	Notes
12:30-12:40	Collaborative Culture, Reflective Thinking	Reflective Icebreaker: Partners in Turn – Complete the sentence: "The underlying belief that I have of _____ about thinking, changed when _____."	2	PLP Facilitator	How can I connect my beliefs and assumptions about teaching and learning to my effectiveness in teaching?	• Journaling	• Reflective teaching	• Week Three Partner • Stand and talk • Five minutes per person
12:40-2:00	Training for Skill Development	A Balanced Literacy Approach: Applying Running Records in Reading (Part II)	2	Consultant F (External)	How can using running records to enhance reading skills in students move me to higher levels of learning?	• Completing a running record followed by coaching with feedback	• Teaching intentionally and explicitly	
2:00-2:15		Break						• Reconvene in grade-level groups
2:15-3:30	Training for Skill Developing	**Teaching for Tomorrow: Preparing for the Future** • Review acquisition lesson design and elements • Use Curriculum Feedback Form (Worksheet 6.3). Indicate strengths and "not-yets" of the grade-level curriculum you've been using in the PLP • Recorder makes notes • Reporter summarizes for the large group	2	Coaches	How can I write a standards-based skill-specific lesson that has clearly written activities which will inspire both teachers and students to greater levels of achievement?	• Developing a week's worth of lessons collaboratively	• Model lessons	• Grade-level groups • Five teachers per group • Brainstorming • Recorder and reporter

119

Figure 6.5: Preview Learning

Staff Development Agenda for Teachers, Coaches, and Administrators

12:00 – 4:00

Week Three, Thursday

(Continued)

Site Code: 1 = Individual School
2 = Staff Development Center
3 = Individual Option

Time	Staff Development Design	Topic	Site	Leader or Facilitator	Guiding Question	Follow-up Staff Development	Expected Outcome(s)	Notes
3:30–4:00	Writing Lessons Collaboratively	**Advance organizer:** Distribute partially completed lesson writing forms and present idea that tomorrow's time in site-specific afternoon lab sessions will be spent collaboratively in writing activities for the missing components	2	Coaches	How can I write a standards-based, skill specific lesson that has clearly written activities which will inspire both teachers and students to greater levels of achievement?	• Teach from lessons that have been written collaboratively with feedback coaching to follow	• Ability to effectively plan and write an acquisition lesson	• Distribute lessons that are partially scaffolded out

Figure 6.5: Preview Learning

Staff Development Agenda for Teachers, Coaches, and Administrators
12:00 – 4:00
Week Three, Friday

Site Code: 1 = Individual School
2 = Staff Development Center
3 = Individual Option

Time	Staff Development Design	Topic	Site	Leader or Facilitator	Guiding Question	Follow-up Staff Development	Expected Outcome(s)	Notes
12:30-12:45	Journaling, Reflection	Write in the Think Book. Complete the sentence: "The underlying belief that I have of _____ about planning lessons has been challenged by _____."	1	School Administrator	How can my learning increase the learning of my students?	• Coaching	• Real-time planning of lessons	• Individuals independently writing within the large group setting
12:45-1:05	Collaborative Discussion	Share specific insights you got as you wrote in your journal.	1	School Administrator with coach charting specific insights			• Collaborative culture	• Look for patterns in the insights as they are verbalized
1:05-1:15		Break						• Reconvene in grade-level groups
1:15-3:45	Writing Lessons Collaboratively	• Discuss the short-term goal for the students in the PLP • Collaboratively complete the summarizing section of each of the Strands for Week Four, staying true to the acquisition lesson design	1	Coaches	How can teachers develop stronger networks with each other so that they can better use each other's knowledge?	• Coaching with feedback	• Increase content knowledge and pedagogical knowledge as teachers discuss the best standards-based activities, solve problems and discuss teaching and learning, and analyze students' thinking • Know more about the students, subject matter, and their own teaching and learning	• Coach circulates to trouble-shoot and offer guidance as needed • The summarizing activities during morning teaching labs will be different at every school as a result of this scaffolding activity
3:45-4:00	Summarizing	Answer three questions: Know what? (What have I learned?) So what? (Why is my learning important?) Now what? (How will I change my teaching as a result of my new learning?)	1	Coaches	How can we use the new knowledge that we have?			• Write in Think Book

121

Figure 6.5: Preview Learning

Staff Development Agenda for Teachers, Coaches, and Administrators

12:00 – 4:00

Week Four, Monday

Site Code: 1 = Individual School
2 = Staff Development Center
3 = Individual Option

Time	Staff Development Design	Topic	Site	Leader or Facilitator	Guiding Question	Follow-up Staff Development	Expected Outcome(s)	Notes
12:30-12:40	Collaborative Culture, Analyzing Instruction	Reflective Icebreaker: Partners in turn – Complete the sentence: "The summarizing activity that I used with my students this morning focused on learning by _____."	2	PLP Facilitator	How can I apply what I have learned to date in the PLP to help me be instruction-ally effective?	• Journaling	• Reflective teaching	• Week four partner • Stand and talk • Five minutes per person
12:40-2:00	Training for Skill Development	Excelling in reading, spelling, and writing	2	Consultant G (Internal: A teacher from the district with expertise in the topic)	How can learning strategies be designed and infused across the strands to provide balanced literacy instruction?	• Lab-based instruction with students followed by feedback coaching	• Explicit and intentional teaching through differentiated instruction	
2:00-2:15		Break						• Reconvene in grade-level groups
2:15-3:50	Writing Lessons Collaboratively	• Collaboratively write a generalization for all strands for Tuesday's lessons. Convert the generalizations to essential questions for the day on which all agree • Review and discuss potential "bumps" in the teaching of the remainder of the strands for Tuesday	2	Coaches monitor and give cues and offer feed-back as needed	How can I capture the essence of what strategic teachers do to help students make sense of what they read?	• Lab-based instruction with students followed by feedback coaching	• Explicit and intentional teaching • Ability to construct relevant essential questions	All grade-level specific teachers use the same essential questions for each strand tomorrow
3:50-4:00	Evaluation	Comment Cards – Complete the sentence: "My feelings about the work I have done on essential questions are _____ because I know that _____."	2	Advance organizer: All four strands for Thursday's lessons will be planned and written by teachers with all the components scaffolded out except the skills and essential questions.				• Coaches collect and review for coaching options

122

Figure 6.5: Preview Learning

Staff Development Agenda for Teachers, Coaches, and Administrators
12:00 – 4:00
Week Four, Tuesday

Site Code: 1 = Individual School
2 = Staff Development Center
3 = Individual Option

Time	Staff Development Design	Topic	Site	Leader or Facilitator	Guiding Question	Follow-up Staff Development	Expected Outcome(s)	Notes
12:30-12:40	Collaborative Culture, Subject-Specific Content	Reflective Icebreaker: Partners in turn—Complete the sentence: "When I used the guided reading strategies that we learned, I found _____."	2	PLP Facilitator	How can I apply what I have learned to date in the PLP to help me be instructionally effective?	• Journaling	• Reflective teaching	• Week four partner • Stand and talk • Five minutes per person
12:40-2:00	Training for Skill Development	Closing the Gap With Visual Tools, Graphic Organizers, and Cognitive Organizers (Part I)	2	Consultant H (Internal: A teacher from the district with expertise in the topic)	How can I help our students understand and retain the concepts behind the facts in such a way that it is motivational to them and me?	• Lab-based instruction with students followed by feedback coaching	• Explicit and intentional teaching of thinking skills	
2:00-2:15		Break						• Reconvene in grade-level groups
2:15-3:50	Writing Lessons Collaboratively	• Collaboratively write a summarizing activity for all strands for the lessons on Wednesday • Review and discuss potential "bumps" in the teaching of the remaining strands for Thursday	2	Coaches	How can I capture the essence of what strategic teachers do to help students make sense of what they read?	• Lab-based instruction with students followed by feedback coaching	• Explicit and intentional teaching • Ability to construct relevant summarizing activities	All grade-level specific teachers use a common grade-level summarizing activity for each of the four strands tomorrow
3:50-4:00	Evaluation	Comment Cards. Complete the sentence: "My feeling about the work I have done with summarizing activities for tomorrow is _____."	2	Coaches				Coaches collect and review with administrators for coaching options

Figure 6.5: Preview Learning

Staff Development Agenda for Teachers, Coaches, and Administrators
12:00 – 4:00
Week Four, Wednesday

Site Code: 1 = Individual School
2 = Staff Development Center
3 = Individual Option

Time	Staff Development Design	Topic	Site	Leader or Facilitator	Guiding Question	Follow-up Staff Development	Expected Outcome(s)	Notes
12:30-12:40	Collaborative Culture, Subject-Specific Content	Reflective Icebreaker: Partners in turn – Complete sentence: "Because I have participated in the staff development activities in the PLP, when I teach in the regular school year I will _____."	2	PLP Facilitator	How can I apply what I have learned to date in the PLP to help me be instructionally effective?	• Journaling	• Reflective teaching	• Week four partner • Stand and talk • Five minutes per person
12:40-2:00	Training for Skill Development	Literary Devices: Visual Tools to Teach Personification, Similes, and Metaphors (Part II)	2	Consultant H (Internal – Continued from Tuesday)	How can I help our students understand and retain concepts behind the facts in a way that is motivational to them and me?	• Lab-based instruction with students followed by feedback coaching	• Explicit and intentional teaching of thinking skills	
2:00-2:15		Break						• Reconvene in grade-level groups
2:15-3:50	Writing Lessons Collaboratively	• Collaboratively plan the lesson to be taught tomorrow by using a Flow Map (a specific Thinking Map). Write prompts for yourself on your copy of the lessons' Flow Charts.	2	Coaches	How can I focus on the questions and prompts essential to teaching and deepen my understanding of tools available for constructing content knowledge necessary for improving student learning?	• Lab-based instruction with students followed by feedback coaching	• The use of a visual tool to bring efficiency, clarity, and equity to what is important in a lesson	
3:50-4:00	Evaluation	Comment Card. Evaluate the morning's teaching episodes. Select an appropriate visual tool to display your thinking.	2	Coach				• Coaches collect and review with the administrator for coaching options

Figure 6.5: Preview Learning

Staff Development Agenda for Teachers, Coaches, and Administrators

12:00 – 4:00

Week Four, Thursday

Site Code: 1 = Individual School
2 = Staff Development Center
3 = Individual Option

Time	Staff Development Design	Topic	Site	Leader or Facilitator	Guiding Question	Follow-up Staff Development	Expected Outcome(s)	Notes
12:30-1:00	Collaborative Culture, Reflection	Reflective Icebreaker: Staff discussion using the sentence stem: "When I taught the lesson this morning that we collaboratively created I learned _____ ."	1	School coach as recorder (Share information with the PLP design team)	How can we get learning to become an explicit focus in conversations with other teachers?	• Journaling	• Reflective teaching • Associating teacher thinking with higher-order thinking skills	• Record your response to topic sentence and guiding question in your Think Book
1:00-2:30	Collaborative Culture	Group Reflection With a Visual Tool • Tool I: The Bubble Map: • Describe the attribute for the lessons you taught today by using a Bubble Map • Tool II: The Double Bubble Map: Compare and contrast the adult teaching and learning activities in which you have participated in the afternoon lab sessions to the activities that you have used in teaching your PLP classroom. Use the Double Bubble Map to display your thinking	1	Coach as encourager and recorder	How can I stimulate conversation that leads to improvement in my teaching?		• Reflective teaching • Engaging in higher-order thinking on a day-to-day basis in the classroom	• Teachers record their work in their Think Book
2:30-2:45		Break						
2:45-3:45	Collaborative Culture	Share selected items from student portfolios, and tell the comments the students made. Look for patterns across the grades.	1	Administrator			• A reversal of under-achievement in literacy among learners caught in the achievement gap	• Note patterns in Think Book
3:45-4:00		Closing that is a site-specific celebration	1	Administrator and Coach				

Figure 6.5: Preview Learning
Staff Development Agenda for Teachers, Coaches, and Administrators

Celebration Day
12:00 – 4:00
Week Four, Friday

Site Code: 1 = Individual School
2 = Staff Development Center
3 = Individual Option

Time	Staff Development Design	Topic	Site	Leader or Facilitator	Guiding Question	Follow-up Staff Development	Expected Outcome(s)	Notes
12:30–1:00	Collaborative Culture, Subject-Specific Content	Reflective Icebreaker: Partners in Turn – Complete the sentence: "I think that one of the keys to success in teaching reading is _____ because _____."	2	PLP Facilitator	How can I apply what I have learned to date in the PLP to help me continue to be instructionally effective?		• Focus on future teaching • A self-reflective teacher who is aware of metacognitive processes	• Week four partner
1:00–2:00	Collaborative Culture, Reflection, Evaluation	Carousel Story: Place seven large sheets of butcher paper at intervals around the room on the walls. Put one question at the top of each page. • What was the most significant benefit of the PLP to me as a learner? • How did I change remediation for students to mediation through preview learning? • Give one strength and one "not-yet" of the curriculum. • The various effects that my teaching has had on student learning include: • Feedback coaching includes the concept of stretching the learner a bit farther during each successful event. The ways that I was stretched as a learner include: • I think the teaching moves of an effective teacher include: • My biggest question about my teaching practice is: • In my teaching, I want to learn more about:	2	PLP Facilitator: Number of participants so you have eight groups of equitable size. Each group will collaboratively answer the question with one person recording the answers. Groups travel clockwise at the sound of the whistle.			• Place a marker at each station of the Carousel Story
2:00–2:15	Break							
2:15–2:45		Read and Review. Rotate around the Carousel Story a second time. Read what others have written. Add more answers if you have them.		PLP Facilitator				• Save Carousel Story for the PLP Design Team

Figure 6.5: Preview Learning
Staff Development Agenda for Teachers, Coaches, and Administrators
12:00 – 4:00
Week Four, Friday
(Continued)

Celebration Day

Site Code: 1 = Individual School
2 = Staff Development Center
3 = Individual Option

Time	Staff Development Design	Topic	Site	Leader or Facilitator	Guiding Question	Follow-up Staff Development	Expected Outcome(s)	Notes
2:45-3:00		Repeat Review. Make one quick rotation again to read all responses.	2	PLP Facilitator				
3:00-3:30		Celebration Story. Folks will stand in a circle. Begin the story by using the phrase, "Once upon a time a group of teachers met in a PLP with students in _____." At that point pass it on to the person on the right. Every person will add a phrase (or phrases) that is relevant to what has happened during this four week period, until everyone around the circle has participated. This story can be drawn to a conclusion as appropriate after all have participated.	2	PLP Facilitator				
3:30-4:00	Reflection, Closing	Carousel Reflection. Place six large pieces of paper on the floor. Each will have one number from 1 up through the number 6. Write one of each of these six questions on each of the papers in large print: • When you applied to teach in this program, what were your expectations? • What advice will you have for teachers applying to participate next year? • How are you better prepared to teach during the regular school year? • How do you see yourself as a learner? • How have you seen your students grow? • How do you see staff development differently now?	2	PLP Facilitator. Number off by sixes. Teachers begin by standing on their number. Teachers read the question silently and reflect on it covertly. As each question is completed, teachers will move in sequential order to the next numbered question. After all six questions have been answered, each teacher goes to a seat and writes one last sentence in the Think Book to summarize his or her experience.				

127

Figure 6.6   Job-Embedded Staff Development

The following activities are selected options that may be used at any time for job-embedded staff development. Others are available as appropriate.

- Discuss student work with another teacher, feedback coach, or administrator.
- Examine personal effectiveness in teaching a skill, and identify the specific need for professional learning to accommodate that skill.
- Discuss informally how your work is aligning with the goals of the PLP and those of the district.
- Serve as a mentor to a colleague.
- Examine the impact of your teaching on student learning.
- Explain to someone else how what you are doing in your teaching will increase the learning for the students in your class.
- Promote the importance of the learning activities in which you are engaged to a colleague.
- Examine for yourself the professional benefit that you are receiving from your involvement in the PLP.
- Collaborate with colleagues about instruction, curriculum, and assessment.
- Work with a learning team to solve an instructional problem.
- Use the baseline student data that you received to monitor improvement across the program.
- Identify changes in student learning.
- Review what constitutes reliable and valid research.
- Give and receive feedback in order to implement new instructional practices.
- Participate in multiple experiences with a coach in which the use of new practices is your goal.
- Adapt new strategies to match classroom circumstances.
- Use knowledge of strategies to monitor and improve group interactions.
- Use effective interaction skills when working with colleagues.
- Use a variety of instructional strategies that motivate all students to learn.
- Exhibit a deep understanding of the concepts that underlie the content or subject matter and successfully integrate them into the PLP lesson.
- Differentiate instruction.
- Ask yourself the following questions on a regular basis: What questions do I ask myself? What assumptions do I have about children and learning? Am I consistent and persistent in communicating my assumptions? Do my questions focus on achievement? What do I monitor? How am I staying relevant in my chosen field?

SOURCE: Adapted from: Roy, P. and Hord, S. (Proj. Dir), 2003. *Moving NSDC's Staff Development Standards into Practice: Innovation Configurations.* Oxford, OH: NSDC.

Figure 6.7   Morning Lab-Based Schedule

8:00–11:00	Preview Learning Instructional Labs for students held at 10 inner-city sites
11:00–11:30	Site-specific planning and administrative time
11:30–12:30	Lunch and travel time to staff development center
12:30–4:00	Preview Learning Instructional Labs for educators

EVALUATING PROFESSIONAL DEVELOPMENT

All the components and activities that make up the complex program of the PLP must be evaluated, because it "is necessary to determine their quality and to gain direction in efforts to improve them" (Guskey, 2000). The section that you are reading now on evaluation is included in this chapter to show that evaluation is always included in the staff development domain; however, the specifics of the evaluation activities that are used in this program will be explained in more detail in Chapter 7.

EXPECTED OUTCOMES FOR STAFF DEVELOPMENT

The long-term goal of the professional development component for the PLP in William's district is to have educators take responsibility for their own learning and the learning of those around them. Meeting the learning needs of students caught in the achievement gap by actively participating in professional learning opportunities is both a short-term and a long-term goal. Therefore, every event discussed in this chapter was explicitly designed to achieve these two goals.

Once the teachers have completed the 22 days of the standards-based, professional learning component of the PLP, they should be motivated to continue to work on a manageable set of new practices in a sustained way over time. This allows them to develop an effective and fairly stable repertoire of teaching practices. Feedback coaching, administrative dialogue, and collegial interaction during the program should allow teachers to develop a feeling of comfort for engaging in new forms of practice in the presence of other people who have some expertise in a given practice. Finally, it is hoped that the teachers in the PLP will find themselves working during the regular school year in schools where reflectivity is integrated into organizational practice. A school with a teacher on its staff who was a faculty member in the PLP will reap the rewards of enhanced learning for all levels of students because of the level of personal and professional growth that the teacher takes to the classroom every day. William's district found this to be true.

MAKING IT "LIVE" FOR YOU: A PLANNING TEMPLATE

1. This is your call to action. Examine the types of staff development that you offer in your district that assist teachers in developing the knowledge and skills necessary to teach a given subject effectively. Confine your investigation to one school year's time. Identify your subject area, and list the staff development opportunities. If there was a follow-up in the program to bridge the gap to excellence, put a check mark in the box to the right of the event. Expand the template as needed as you work.

Subject Area You Are Examining

Content-driven Staff Development   *Opportunities in Your District*

Activity   *Date*   *Follow-up*

_____

_____

_____

_____

_____

2. For your own information, describe the core reading curriculum in your district.

3. Visit the Web site of the National Staff Development Council (www.nsdc.org) and review the Standards for Staff Development, Revised. Select one of the Content Standards and compare and contrast your core reading curriculum using the guide in Worksheet 6.1 (see page 196 in the Resources).

4. Think about an explicit strategic intervention (Fullan, 1999) that you can develop (or one on which you are currently working) to meet a need in your system. Examine how you can immerse educators in a new learning experience by developing questions that reinforce the fact that the professional development design will be about the desired learning for students. Review the questions presented earlier in this chapter and then write your questions here.

5. Develop a comprehensive agenda to help you achieve your desired outcome. Use the template in Worksheet 6.2 (see page 197 in the Resources) to help you design your blueprint for growth.

6. The Staff Development Agenda lists (in the Week Three, Thursday, section) a need for a Curriculum Feedback Form to investigate the strengths and "not-yets" of the grade-level curriculum. It is shown in Worksheet 6.3 (see page 198 in the Resources) for your use.

7

Assessing for Effectiveness

Evaluating Quality

*The formula is well known, now all we need is to
follow it.*

—Mike Schmoker

ESTABLISHING THE EVALUATION FRAMEWORK

The evaluation framework in William's district was designed early in the program's planning to give direction to the design team. This advance work helped the group formulate the components of the Preview Learning Program (PLP) and determine strategic ways to assess effectiveness. Numerous evaluation designs were examined, leading to the decision that the team would adopt no single model for evaluation. The use of both quantitative and qualitative information that was specific to the program would be used, however, to guide them in developing each component effectively. Questionnaires, surveys, tests, and existing databases (quantitative), along with observations, interviews, and focus questions (qualitative) needed to be included in the overall design in order to determine answers to the numerous evaluation questions that had emerged during the frequent brainstorming sessions. Knowing that qualitative and qualitative methods each have different strengths, weaknesses, and requirements in design work, the team designed the evaluation framework of the PLP to include a variety of methodologies that would give them good feedback.

Figure 7.1 Evaluation Framework

Program Goal: To improve student reading at the elementary level

Measurable Objectives:

- Students enrolled in the PLP will perform better than the control group on the Unit I reading tests during the regular school year.
- Twenty percent of the PLP students will score proficient or above on the Standardized Total Reading Test during year one of the program.
- Students in classes taught during the regular school year by teachers who taught in the PLP will perform better on measures of reading ability than their peers incomparable classrooms.
- Teachers' attitudes toward struggling readers will change after teaching in the PLP.

Information and Timeline:

- List of participants (students and educators) in the PLP (August)
- List of control group of students (September)
- PLP students' total reading scores for the two previous years (August)
- PLP teachers' Standardized Total Reading results compared to comparable students' scores from the non-PLP teachers (May)
- Survey of teacher attitudes about the impact they have directly on the low-achieving student (August and May)
- Survey of student level of confidence in reading (First day of PLP and again in October)
- Survey of level of use of instructional practice during regular school year (February)
- Feedback from teachers on the PLP curriculum and instructional strategies (end of PLP session and February)

Data Sources:

- Standardized Total Reading scores of target and control groups
- Basal Reader Unit Test for the PLP teachers and control teachers
- Teacher survey – attitude and level of implementation
- Student attitudinal survey (first day of PLP with follow-up in the fall)
- Observations by coaches for level of use of effective strategies
- District and school records
- Student portfolios
- Minutes from teacher discussions
- Teachers' reflections on teaching and student work
- Structured interviews with teachers and their administrators and coaches

---

Figure 7.1 shows the evaluation framework that the design committee developed for the PLP.

EVALUATING THE JOURNEY

Guskey (2000) reminds us that formative evaluation can be used as an early version of the final, overall evaluation. Inclusion of the process allows individuals and design teams to critically examine and analyze their daily work to determine what is working as expected, and to identify what needs to be looked at for flaws and weaknesses. Joellen Killion (2003) uses the term *evaluation think* to describe this process. She encourages its use by saying that evaluation think does not have to be complicated. It can be simple in style, but it must be intentional in focus. Schmoker (2002) adds that the process must also include strong improvement mechanisms. The team in William's district liked the concept of evaluation think and infused opportunities for the use of the process throughout the PLP. Evaluation think will be the main ingredient in the program's framework to inform the design team if the lab-based model reached the goal of using powerful staff development to improve student reading. Figure 7.2 shows the formative assessment index for the PLP. The index uses existing records, extra surveys developed to ascertain immediate need, instruments designed specifically for the PLP, and other strategies to help answer the question, "How are we doing in achieving our goal?"

The index contains 27 separate items. Each tool serves a unique assessment purpose. As you peruse the list, you will note that many of the items have been discussed in previous chapters. An asterisk has been placed after each of these items for easy identification. The remaining items in the list are described in more detail below.

AMPLIFYING FORMATIVE ASSESSMENT TOOLS

Tool One: Student Survey

A student attitudinal survey was designed to determine if the students improved in the way they felt about reading by the end of the four-week PLP. Since low achievers typically say they don't like reading because they find the task difficult, the survey was given on the first day of the PLP. In an intervention program like the PLP, it is expected that students' attitudes about participating in reading classes should improve and their efficacy should increase as they achieve success in reading. To determine if this assumption is actually true, the same survey was given again during the fall of the regular school year following the students' participation in the PLP. The design team fully expects the survey to show a change in both students' attitude and aspirations. Hopefully, the survey will indicate that the participating students will want to become even better in reading than they are now; understand the importance of success in school; and even express a desire to be more successful in their schoolwork. The student survey in Figure 7.3 was used in William's district to gather this informative data.

Tool Two: Teacher Survey

The theory of change for student learning and professional growth through a lab-based design states that because teachers participate in learning experiences, they will use their new learning to increase students' academic knowledge; thus, student learning and performance increase. Just as students

Figure 7.2   Formative Assessment Index

Event	Formative Assessment
Curriculum development	• Curriculum rubric* • Assessment rubric • Acquisition lesson design*
Teacher, Administrator, Coach selection	• What teachers should know and be able to do* • Qualifying questionnaire* • Rank-order selection process*
Student selection	• Review of district level data* • Developmental timeline for program* • School-specific student selection* • Administrator and teacher feedback* • Site registration*
Instructional design	• Instruction rubric* • Administrator walk-through
Staff development	• Structured daily reflection* • Journal writing • Practice with coaching • Instruction rubric • Lab-based training* • Collegial sharing* • Coaching
Student and teacher learning	• Teacher observation • Student portfolios • Student records* • School records* • Student survey • Teacher survey • Principal walk-through

NOTE: *Discussed in previous chapters

have attitudes and concerns about their learning, so do educators. When teachers have a concern of any kind about students in their classes learning or not learning to read, it may be reflected in their attitudes about teaching reading and the use of motivational strategies in their subsequent instruction of the subject. In view of this fact, it is hypothesized here that teachers who are reluctant to teach reading (even though they may be "good" teachers) use fewer effective instructional strategies for the subject, and therefore are less

Figure 7.3   Student Survey

Directions: Put a check mark under the Yes or No to show the way you feel at this time about the statement.

	Yes	No
• Reading is my favorite subject.		
• I enjoy listening to stories being read.		
• I read at home for fun.		
• I am a good reader.		
• I like reading to others.		
• I want to become a better reader.		
• Practice will make me a better reader.		
• Reading will help me in life.		
• I learn about things in reading.		
• Reading is easy for me.		
• Reading helps me get good grades.		

effective in motivating students to achieve. To determine if a lab-based design would have an impact on this hypothesis, the design team in William's district chose to develop and administer a teacher survey. It was used as a pretest and posttest to determine changes, if any, in teachers' attitudes due to being involved in a quality program with powerful learning components. Effective instructional strategies, used strategically, should increase student learning. Figure 7.4 shows the pretest and posttest that were designed to give the team in William's district the feedback it needed.

Tool Three: Student Portfolio

An alternative to a traditional test, the student portfolio is a qualitative performance assessment that shows the ongoing and developmental impact the program is having on an individual student. The formative assessment plan directs that each portfolio will include significant and purposeful work samples. The student and teacher should collaboratively select the contents at several points during the PLP and together assess the quality of each product in light of the guidelines given to the teacher, the essential question for the day of choice, and the goal of the PLP. The actual performance of the student should provide information on the impact of the curriculum and instructional strategies on the student's learning.

Figure 7.4   Teacher Survey

1. What is your assignment for next year?
   - ○ regular classroom teacher
   - ○ special education teacher
   - ○ guidance counselor
   - ○ physical education teacher
   - ○ media specialist
   - ○ educational specialist
   - ○ other_____

2. How long have you been an educator?
   - ○ less than 3 years
   - ○ 3 to 5 years
   - ○ 6 to 10 years
   - ○ 11 to 20 years
   - ○ more than 20 years

3. If you are a regular classroom teacher, what grade do you teach?
   - ○ K
   - ○ 1st
   - ○ 2nd
   - ○ 3rd
   - ○ 4th
   - ○ 5th

Please indicate the degree to which you agree or disagree with each statement.

	Strongly Agree	Tend to Agree	Tend to Disagree	Strongly Disagree
4. Reading is the most important subject I teach.	○	○	○	○
5. I find it easy to motivate students to learn how to read.	○	○	○	○
6. A child's reading ability largely determines his/her success in other subjects.	○	○	○	○
7. Every child can become a proficient reader.	○	○	○	○
8. My instructional strategies meet the academic needs of every child in my classroom.	○	○	○	○

Reflect on your reading instruction during the past year. Classify the following instructional grouping patterns with (1) being more frequently used and (3) being less frequently used.

a. total group	1	2	3
b. small group	1	2	3
c. cooperative learning groups	1	2	3
d. partner learning/peer tutoring	1	2	3
e. individualized one-on-one	1	2	3

Again reflect on your reading instruction during the past year. From the following list, classify the instructional strategies based on how frequently you used them with (1) being the more frequently used and (3) being less frequently used.

Classification

a.	activating thinking	1	2	3
b.	checking for understanding	1	2	3
c.	decoding	1	2	3
d.	graphic organizers	1	2	3
e.	guided reading	1	2	3
f.	modeling	1	2	3
g.	predict/verify	1	2	3
h.	reader response journals	1	2	3
i.	round robin reading	1	2	3
j.	shared reading	1	2	3
k.	shared writing	1	2	3
l.	summarizing	1	2	3

One of the primary goals of staff development is to positively impact student achievement. Consider the components of the Preview Learning Program's staff development. Classify their impact on student achievement with (1) being highly effective and (3) being ineffective.

Effectiveness

a.	assessment	1	2	3
b.	guided reading	1	2	3
c.	vocabulary development	1	2	3
d.	writing	1	2	3
e.	reading in content area (grades 3–5)	1	2	3
f.	word study (grades K–2)	1	2	3

The portfolios in each class were structured for student success in the PLP. To help achieve this success, the teachers used the following guidelines:

1. Optional containers for portfolios

   - Zipper bag
   - Looseleaf notebook
   - Report folder
   - Portable file case
   - Decorated box
   - Video (as a container of media, or audio-visual, work)
   - Folded construction paper

2. Optional portfolio cover

   - Shows a motif of literature that has been a theme throughout the PLP
   - Expresses something about the person who created the portfolio
   - States the owner's name

3. Table of contents

4. Graphics. The portfolio should be visually appealing.

5. Self-evaluation. Note the following two items.

- Each selection that is included should have an attached, written comment where the student finishes *one* of the following thoughts about his work:

  ○ This piece did not work for me because . . .
  ○ This piece was a stretch for me because . . .
  ○ This piece gave me a new insight into _____ because . . .
  ○ People who knew me last year would not believe this piece because . . .
  ○ This piece shows how I have met my target goal because . . .
  ○ This piece shows that I have a great deal to learn about ____ because . . .
  ○ This piece shows my growth in reading because . . .
  ○ If I could do this lesson again, I would . . .

For younger students who have difficulty articulating their thoughts, a simple index card may be attached with a drawing the students do to express their self-evaluation.

- Select one item that is not going to be included in the portfolio, and record on a cassette tape why it is not included. This information is important to the program evaluation, because it can help improve subsequent professional development programs and activities that will be planned for future PLPs.

Note that William's portfolio was objective and reflected his learning from day to day. His portfolio was in a pizza box, which he had decorated with pictures that he drew of his family. The pictures included his mother and father along with his younger brother, Thomas, and baby sister, Shelly. The self-evaluation statement that he completed the most was "*People who knew me last year would not believe this piece because . . . !*" William was developing pride in his work.

Tool Four: Level-of-Use Rubric

Rubrics are effective tools to strengthen a design, because they feed information back to team members in ways that help them pay closer attention to desired outcomes. In the PLP, rubrics were used in the initial planning stages to

- Guide the design team in strategic ways
- Help the team infuse opportunities for formative assessment into the program's design
- Prescribe a minimum level of use of formative assessment in the instructional component

Figure 7.5   Formative Assessment Rubric: Level of Use

Level One	The main mode of assessment consists of end-of-day questions, paper-and-pencil activities, and/or memory tests that may not reinforce or develop skills that are aligned with the essential question.
Level Two	The assessment system sometimes is separate from instruction. Feedback is given but it is focused on the student, not the essential task, and one tool is used during the program's duration to assess learning.
Level Three	The assessment system uses a number of tools to assess for learning, paying attention to literalness, repetition, and supported assessment. The teacher gives feedback based on the essential question.
Level Four	The assessment system is committed to promoting literal skills, progress through repetition, and supported assessment. A number of tools to assess for learning are used. The teachers give feedback based on the essential question, give the students an opportunity to express their understanding of the feedback, and provide opportunities for students to self-assess.

- Plan evaluation of the newly written curriculum and instructional strategies
- Assist administrators with the quality of their classroom walk-throughs

Throughout the program, the use of rubrics in William's district was focused on improving student learning. Figure 7.5 shows the rubric on the Level of Use of Formative Assessment, which the team developed as an assessment tool to guide the distribution of assessment activities that were employed in the program's design.

ASSESSING AS STAFF DEVELOPMENT

Expertise can be cultivated; therefore, the PLP design team in William's district began with the premise that good teachers can best facilitate academic learning for the substantial numbers of children caught in the achievement gap. The team noted that there were many teachers in the district demonstrating that they could differentiate instruction based on interest and background. They could even write exciting lesson plans, and all of them had good scores in their state's regular teacher evaluation system. Most of them, however, could not match strategy to need, articulate why they chose the instructional strategies they did, elaborate on specific content or learning objectives (Roy & Hord, 2003), or tell how to incorporate content, standards, or effective formative assessment into their work.

Acquiring the skill necessary to accomplish each of these tasks will make a good teacher better and normalize the skill across the district—just what was needed in William's district. Each of these skills is an important part of evaluation think and must be included in the evaluation and assessment domain of a Preview Learning Program. It will require a focus on each element and much hard work to accomplish this, because none of it will happen magically. It is possible to have parity in this, however, if a quality staff development component is offered to help all educators amplify their learning.

William's district linked staff development and assessment in the PLP. The team wanted teachers to have a deeper understanding of teaching as a complex task and to understand that it demands sophisticated intellectual and interpersonal skills. To do this, they made a move to

- Help teachers critically examine their learning through doing
- Reflect on their work
- Work collaboratively in teams
- Have personal and interpersonal accountability

The strategies used to accomplish this are explained here. The implementation of these strategies is discussed in Chapter 6. The focus in this chapter is their fit in the evaluation domain. The tight alignment of the strategies described here and the activities included in Chapter 6 show that there is no separating evaluation and staff development where student learning is involved.

Strategy One: Peer Coaching

Peer coaching is a "confidential process in which two or more professional colleagues work together to reflect on current practices; expand, refine, and build new skills; share ideas; and solve problems that arise in the program" (Robbins, 1991). The purpose of coaching is to expand the resources of individual teachers so that they can better serve students. An effective, job-embedded professional learning structure, coaching is used in the PLP to focus on activities such as instructional strategies (Marzano, Pickering, & Pollack, 2001); curriculum content; assessment practices; specific students or problems; or conversation about student work (Robbins, 2004; Schlechty, 2001). The main focus is on the teacher as a learner.

The cognitive coaching approach was used mostly in developing the coaching component for the PLP, because the definition of the process is congruent with this intervention program. Costa and Garmston (1990) define cognitive coaching as *"a set of strategies, a way of thinking, and a way of working that invites self and others to shape and reshape their thinking and problem solving capacities."*

In William's district, an external consultant helped all the program's staff understand the purpose of coaching and learn how to implement the process

Figure 7.6   Feedback Coach: Basic Follow-up Questions

- What did your students learn today? How do you know?

- What student behaviors did you observe to indicate to you that your lesson was successful?

- If you could repeat today's lesson again tomorrow to a different group of students with the same abilities, how might you do it differently within the structure that has been given to you?

- What do you need from me at this time?

in a nonthreatening way. Questioning became the strategy of choice for the coaching process. In order to maintain consistency in inquiry, basic questions were developed and given to all staff members in advance. The questions only numbered four (see Figure 7.6), but they were explicit and powerful and designed to help the coach and teacher begin an assessment dialogue. Other questions were asked according to need and opportunity.

In the formative assessment process, the coaches were asked to self-assess about the degree of clarity they achieved with the teacher and his thinking during a specific episode. The following questions, adapted from Costa and Garmston (1990), are reflection questions that were used to guide coaches' thinking.

- How did I elicit feelings from the teacher about the implementation of an event or episode?
- How did I get the teacher to refer to objective data?
- What strategy did I use to elicit an analysis of the data?
- Did I question for deeper understanding? How did I do that?
- What did I learn from my conversation with the teacher?
- What feedback did I receive from the teacher about my skills as a feedback coach? How did I elicit the feedback?
- Based on what I have learned, what suggestions do I have for myself for next time?

The answers to these questions will provide structure for journal writing for each coach and content for dialogue when the coaches get together for group-alike conversations.

Strategy Two: Journal Writing

Structured journal writing is used in the PLP as a formative assessment strategy. The process makes invisible thoughts visible and uses the unpolished writing to engage higher-order intellectual skills such as fluency of thought, analysis of concepts, and inducing from experience, to name only a few. York-Barr, Sommers, Ghere, & Montie (2001) reference Taggart and Wilson (1998) in listing the benefits of journaling as "expanding awareness, understanding, and insights about teaching practice; making connections between theory and practice; and generating new hypotheses for action. It is a valuable

Figure 7.7 Purpose of Principal Walk-Through

The purpose of the principal walk-through in the PLP is:

- To be a reflectional supervisor through a supportive, nurturing relationship (Downey, Steffy, English, Frase & Poston, Jr., 2004).

- To focus on the factors in the PLP's curriculum and instructional strategies that influence high achievement.

- To promote the use of assessment for diagnostic purposes.

- To facilitate teachers collaboratively working with each other in instructional improvement activities.

- To interact with the staff about their practice.

- To increase the knowledge base of the administrator so that he will have a greater repertoire of strategies to share with staff.

- To establish the fact that feedback is a critical component in the learning process.

process for anyone who is serious about ensuring success for all students." The educators in William's district used the practice daily, as indicated in the staff development agendas found in Chapter 6.

Strategy Three: Principal Walk-Through

In the Preview Learning Program, administrators monitor academic focus by conducting brief walk-throughs in classrooms. No conversation takes place between the administrator and teacher while the administrator is in the classroom. The purpose of the walk-through in the PLP is displayed in Figure 7.7.

In the follow-up conversation between the administrator and the teacher, the dialogue is restricted to the evidence of student learning that is visible and self-explanatory as it relates to the essential question of the day. The principal might thumb through a student's portfolio, scan the bulletin board for student work related to the goal, or peep over the shoulder of a student as she is engaged in a learning activity. The principal carries no clipboard or record keeping device that may be threatening to the teacher. If necessary, records or brief notes are jotted down after the administrator exits the room.

Strategy Four: Teacher Observation of Students

The low student-teacher ratio gave teachers the opportunity to observe each student for much of the time they were with them. During their observations, teachers can discern each student's learning style, participation style, and patterns of communication. All these elements are critical to the teacher as he tries to understand the subtle differences among students from diverse backgrounds. In William's district, the teachers were given support in their observations through the use of carefully crafted techniques to involve students in the acquisition lessons at every grade level. The pair-share activities, brain breaks, and collaborative sharing are examples of this.

A responsible learning environment is one where everyone is willing to be held accountable for achieving results. Each of these four strategies can be a catalyst for making this happen.

APPRAISING, JUDGING, AND MEASURING VALUE

"We shouldn't try something better until we first determine if we should do it at all," said 34th U.S. President Dwight D. Eisenhower. This speaks to evaluation. Evaluations are necessary to gain direction for improving the program as it develops, and to determine the program's effectiveness by obtaining evidence of its accomplishments in terms of the goals. We have already explored several ways that the PLP gathered information to determine the extent to which the participants and the program elements were moving toward the goal. Now it is time to find out the following:

- To what extent did the PLP in William's district meet its overall goal?
- Was the PLP effective for both students and teachers?
- What components of the PLP were most effective?
- What components of the program need to be strengthened?

Answers to these four questions come to life in the summative evaluation below.

EVALUATION DESIGN

A mixed-method design is used in evaluating the PLP in William's district, because the evaluation team (district director of research, staff development supervisor, program coordinator, and program supervisors) feels that this method will be more comprehensive and provide a more reliable set of understandings about the PLP's accomplishments (Sharp & Frechtling, 1997), rather than looking at just the quantitative and qualitative data alone (taken from *Designing and Reporting Mixed Methods Evaluations*, www.nsf.gov/pubs/1997/ nsf97153/start.htm). The design team's original plan for combining information from different data sources will be followed as presented. Each technique is germane to the program's goals and objectives.

SUMMATIVE EVALUATION

The summative evaluation includes relevant data from the formative assessment and shows the results of questioning used to guide thinking. The evaluation questions, individual activities used to gather data, type of method used, and sources of information are charted in Figure 7.8 for easy reference. A more complete document, with a narrative on results, is found in Appendix A.

EVALUATION RESULTS

The design team in William's district summarized the results detailed in Appendix A and shared them with all the stakeholders in the district. Information was formally presented to the school board, superintendent, supervisors, and principals. This select group then shared the results with their respective staffs. The district Web site highlighted the results and displayed visual representations of the lab experiences of teachers, along with the collaborative sharing of students.

As a result of the summary, it was determined that if reading scores were to continue to increase, as the data show they did during the summer program, follow-up in the regular school year will be required. This expansion element, properly employed, holds the potential to dramatically alter students' achievement over time. In William's district, the expansion component was offered at individual school sites. Each ingredient of the expansion differed in delivery mode.

EXPANDING THE CONCEPT

One major design modification in the PLP in William's district was made as a result of summarizing the evaluation results and continuing to research what works for students in the achievement gap. Reading scores had increased with the first year's four-week preview learning activities, and PLP teachers were teaching more strategically in their regular classes during the school year. In reality, however, a weakness reappeared in students after the first grading period. That period of grading was the only time when the PLP design included an opportunity for follow-up of the preview instruction and for the students to achieve mastery. The ensuing grading periods during the regular year had no preparation preceding them. If reading scores were to continue to increase, follow-up into the regular school year would be necessary. The design team reviewed the need and saw the plan for moving into the regular school year happening in one of two different ways. Each of these ways is in narrative form in Appendix B and includes three graphic depictions to illustrate each model. The graphics show (1) the PLP's four-week summer design; (2) school year model one; and (3) school year model two.

Expanding preview learning into the school year has the potential to improve student achievement dramatically over time. This sequel definitely contributed to William's success. The program at his school site offered different ingredients and activities than some other school sites, because it was developed to meet student needs specific to that individual and school. The program did not differ in definition. Students who began the journey in the summer continued their trek along the same path to improvement. The site-specific teachers who had been trained in the lab-based summer PLP became the lead teachers (LTs) at the individual expanded sites. They partnered with partner teachers (PTs) who had not participated in the special professional growth opportunities in which

Figure 7.8   Summative Evaluation

Evaluation Question	Activity	Type of Method	Source of Information
I. To what extent did the PLP meet its overall goal for being a force for improved student learning and enhanced leadership and teaching practice?	1. Measure of fall performance	Quantitative	Random sampling
	2. Standardized test	Quantitative	Students enrolled in the PLP
	3. Survey of teacher use of reading strategies in spring of regular school year following the first year of PLP	Quantitative	Random sampling
II. Was the PLP effective for both students and teachers?	1. Reading pretest and posttest	Quantitative	PLP students
	2. Pretest and posttest for writing	Quantitative	PLP students
	3. Student attitude survey during first week and last week of PLP	Quantitative	PLP students
	4. Educator survey of principals, feedback coaches, and grade-level teachers	Quantitative	Random sample
III. What components of the PLP were the most effective? Need to be strengthened?	1. Teacher survey of PLP principals, feedback coaches, and grade-level teachers	Qualitative and quantitative	Random sample
	2. Written educator survey of PLP principals, feedback coaches, and grade-level teachers	Quantitative	Random sample
IV. What reading content and related teaching strategies would teachers like to spend more time learning about in their staff development time?	Survey of PLP principals, feedback coaches, and grade-level teachers	Quantitative	Random sampling

the LT was involved during the special summer program. This collaboration between the teachers encouraged teacher growth in three major ways:

1. The LT modeled new and appropriate skills for the PT. This strengthened the possibility that effective strategies would be used to a greater degree in the school.

2. The PT was motivated to replicate effective strategies in his classroom.

3. The PT increased his skill and boosted his teaching efficacy, which encouraged him to go through the teacher selection process for the summer PLP. In most instances, his short exposure to collaborative work with an LT—and the use of effective strategies on a regular basis—increased the PT's professional knowledge enough that he was successful in the teacher selection process for the summer program. Since one of the stated strengths of the summer PLP includes unique opportunities for teachers to grow professionally, the PT becomes a key part of normalizing effectiveness in teaching throughout the district.

The expansion into the regular school year initiated a cycle of growth for all teachers that continues today. Professional growth opportunities in the expansion phase are not lab-based, however. The process becomes more job-embedded into the routine of the school day and school week. Research tells us that there are ways other than workshops for educators to learn, and that these alternatives offer the potential for improving effectiveness that will lead to improved student learning. A complete list of options for schools and districts may be found on the Web site of the National Staff Development Council (www.nsdc.org). Among the attractive options are analyzing teaching cases; planning lessons with a teaching colleague; keeping a reflective journal; and participating in a study group. Each of the strategies just named, and most of the strategies on the Web site, are integrated into this book. These are the strategies that will lead all educators to change their practice.

MAKING IT "LIVE" FOR YOU: A PLANNING TEMPLATE

1. To verify your understanding of evaluation think, write your definition here and follow up the activity by reviewing Killion's (2003) work with the concept.

_____

_____

_____

_____

2. Schmoker (2002) writes that evaluation must include direct and strong improvement mechanisms. List at least four instruments that you can use in your district to infuse evaluation throughout your framework.

   a. _____

   b. _____

   c. _____

   d. _____

3. Develop an evaluation framework for your program. Use the template provided in Worksheet 7.1, on page 199 in the Resources.

4. Prepare a formative assessment index for your use that references relevant information from records that already exist in your school or district and includes surveys and other instruments that you will develop to present a comprehensive index. Use the template in Worksheet 7.2 (on page 200 of the Resources) to assist you.

5. If you use a student survey in your program design, refer to Figure 7.3 for guidance as needed.

6. A good design for a teacher survey is provided for your adaptation in Figure 7.4. Create your own or adapt this one for your use.

7. Student portfolios need structure to be effective assessment tools. Sentence stems are provided above in Tool Three: Student Portfolio to help you impose your structure. Write the sentence stems here that will enhance student learning through portfolio development for your subject area.

   a. _____

   b. _____

   c. _____

   d. _____

   e. _____

8. Develop a rubric for level of use of formative assessment to guide your planning. Use Worksheet 7.3 on page 201 in the Resources.

9. Questions are important in the process of feedback coaching. Develop your questions for the coaching process on Worksheet 7.4. (See page 202 in the Resources.)

10. The administrator walk-through process will help your school or district focus on factors and strategies that influence high achievement.

Review the process and determine how it could be used in your school or district. Record a statement of purpose about the walk-through process that will serve you on Worksheet 7.5. (See page 203 in the Resources.)

11. Choose one of the models on expanding the concept of Preview Learning into the school year that will work for you in your school or system. The models are presented in Appendix B. Use the blank model in Worksheet 7.6 (see page 204 in the Resources) to assist you in your thinking and decision making. The plan can be flexible, but any extension should join preview and review together as additional elements to regular classroom learning of essential skills and concepts.

8

Summary

Exceeding Expectations

From worst, the best can come.

—Chargi

WILLIAM TODAY

Thomas is William's younger brother. He has an IQ of 98, two points lower than William's, has many of the same hobbies and interests as William, and exhibits many of the same characteristics. There is a three years' difference in their ages. Thomas likes all phases of school and is especially pleased to be sitting in the very same seat, in the very same desk, that William had when he was in this grade. He considers all his classmates to be "good" friends, but the favorite person in the room is his teacher! She is the same teacher that William had when he was in the same grade. That pleases him, too!

His teacher this year is excellent. Thomas saw her walking through the hall in the preview session that he attended last summer. He secretly wished he were in her classroom then, because she had been William's teacher a few years back. He was happy, however, with the teacher he did have last summer. She was very good and helped them "learn" many of the things that he is learning in the regular class now. The teacher smiled and laughed with the seven students in his class and made learning fun, just like his teacher this year. His summer teacher also used much of what she called "graphics," just like the charts he sees William using to help him understand his homework. This year's teacher uses the same "pictures." He likes putting his thinking into the circles, triangles, and rectangles. Both teachers have helped him understand how what he is learning ties to something that he has learned before. Further, each one lets him make a folder to collect special work of his choosing. His teacher this year must have been an actress before she became a teacher! Every time he and his friends get ready to learn how to do something new, she begins to act out exactly how to do the work. She even tells them what she is doing while she acts it out. Her "acting" is so good that when she says she will help them do the same thing, he is able to keep up and follow everything she says and does.

Today is Wednesday, and Thomas is especially eager for reading because he learned in class on Tuesday afternoon, during the daily special focus time called "tomorrow's fun," that one of the things that he and his friends would talk about today is whales. The teacher gave them a "sneak peek" about the lesson and even gave the class two new words, which she promised they would see again today. Further, she asked them to talk about the words at home with a family member of their choosing before they came to school today. Because he idolizes his big brother, Thomas chose William to talk to about his words. William was a good choice, because he has developed into a willing and encouraging listener and conversationalist.

William was silently pleased on Tuesday night when Thomas asked him to listen to his new words. They worked together only a short amount of time when William determined that Thomas was excited about his assignment and very knowledgeable about whales. This fact did not surprise him, because he and Thomas love TV programs about nature, and specifically whales, and watch them often. Their work together on Tuesday night caused William to remember the time that he read the story about whales when he was in school and sat in the seat where Thomas sits this year. He did not, however, remember being excited about reading at that time. In fact, he dreaded the subject because it was so difficult for him to figure out the words. He finds this memory odd now, because he likes reading and other subjects, doesn't mind doing his homework, and looks forward to the many times in class when he and his pals get to work together to discuss ideas. He even finds that he enjoys being the person who is often called on to lead the discussion in his group. How different he feels now. In fact, he marvels silently about the way he has changed his opinion about school. He is amazed at himself, but oh so pleased to be who he is today, and even looks forward to going to school on most days.

Sitting here with Thomas, William cannot help but compare how his current teacher does many of the same things that the summer teacher did when he went to his first special preview session several summers ago. He had gone for only two summers, because he did so well and learned so much. Now that he thinks about it, the teachers in the mini-sessions that he also attended for five days between each of the grading periods during the school year that followed the first preview summer program taught in the same way. His memory turns to one common action that each of his teachers used during the past three years. Each one has written special information on a chart to show the vital skills that he and his friends must learn in order to be able to learn even more information about their current topic. They talked about the essential information in class, had brain breaks with the words and other information, and knew why they were doing what they were doing. On occasion, each teacher would also list important skills on the chart. He is glad that the teacher this year does the same thing. All the teachers let him, and everyone in the class, know that all are special and that they (the teachers) are there to help everyone learn. William believes all of them because of their actions.

William leaves his memories and focuses on what he is doing with Thomas at home, just as Thomas asks William to watch him draw a picture of one of the new words for tomorrow. The last thought he has before looking intently at what Thomas is doing is that having the lists that each teacher makes, and going to extra preview sessions during the regular school year, is probably one of the reasons that he does not mind, and even enjoys, learning new things now. Now he can do anything that most of his friends can do during learning time, and he feels like the "king of the hill" because of it!

MOVING FORWARD: GLANCING BACK

How exciting it is to be able to report that William is one of the students who were included in the system's goal attainment. He still has an IQ of 100, still loves to be around his friends, and is a big sports fan. However, now he knows how to monitor his own learning, is developing leadership skills, and

- Has a high self-efficacy and participates more fully in the process of learning
- Prefers tasks that are moderately challenging, rather than gravitating toward those that are low in degree of difficulty
- Is physically present in the classroom
- Is learning to use logical information-gathering and decision-making strategies
- Knows that when he fails at a task it is because he gave it insufficient effort or lacked information. The "other" William felt that he was not capable when he failed.
- Was in the group of PLP students that showed a mean score of 64.24 at the end of the reading test given during the first PLP session that he attended, as compared to the control group, who showed a mean score of 52.15
- Is out of the achievement gap. Prior to participating in the PLP, William was not among the best students, with his chances in life correspondingly reduced.

William's district is responsible for his success and the success that Thomas—and others like the two of them—will surely experience because the district designed a program to achieve parity in achievement across diverse groups of students. Though complex in design, the simple elegance of the model is its plan to

- Develop high expectations for success in students who have faced repeated failure.
- Ensure students the opportunity to experience a classroom that is caring and supportive.

- Help teachers discover how to use various task dimensions that foster motivation to learn.
- Capitalize on the expertise that existed in the system and build strength from the growth edge outward to new levels of excellence.
- Define congruence between effective curriculum, instruction, assessment, and evaluation, through the lens of job-embedded staff development.

OUR CHALLENGE

We have a challenge and we must meet it. Martin Luther King, Jr. said, "The ultimate measure of a man is not where he stands in moments of comfort and convenience, but where he stands in times of challenge." The measure of our mettle, then, is determined by what we do with the challenge that is before us. If we do all that we know to do, we can inevitably create promising opportunities for each student. We all know more now than we previously knew because of the program developed in William's district and reported here. This information must be used to help us confront our urgent problem with bold and courageous strategies that are proven to work. We are compelled to use it and make it work for each of us. Morally and ethically, we can do no less!

MAKING IT "LIVE" FOR YOU: A PLANNING TEMPLATE

1. Analyze your own school or system in light of the new model presented here for addressing the problems of youngsters in the achievement gap. You have completed the planning templates at the end of each chapter. That information will assist you in doing a summary analysis. Figure 8.1 is provided to assist you in structuring your review. Begin the exercise by identifying components in your school or district that are like the components in the PLP. Place your ideas in the box in the upper left-hand corner of the template. Follow that by noting the differences between the PLP and your school or system in the areas of teacher selection, a purpose-driven curriculum, value-added instruction, staff development based on student learning, assessing for modifications, and evaluating effectiveness. Add more boxes for your work, if necessary. Place the names of the components that you are examining in the middle column of boxes in the lower left-hand corner of the template. The difference in the work that is going on in specific components in your school or system goes in the box on the far left of the lower section on the left-hand side. The differences to which you have compared each component in the PLP go in the boxes on the right-hand side of the diagram, in the lower left-hand quadrant of the page. To complete your analysis, think "Now what?" This means, now that you have read the book, completed your chapter-by-chapter analysis, and compared and contrasted your school or system globally to the PLP, what would you like to do with your analysis and new information? There are places for a beginning plan of action on the right-hand side of the template.

Figure 8.1   A Summer Learning Lab for Students and Teachers

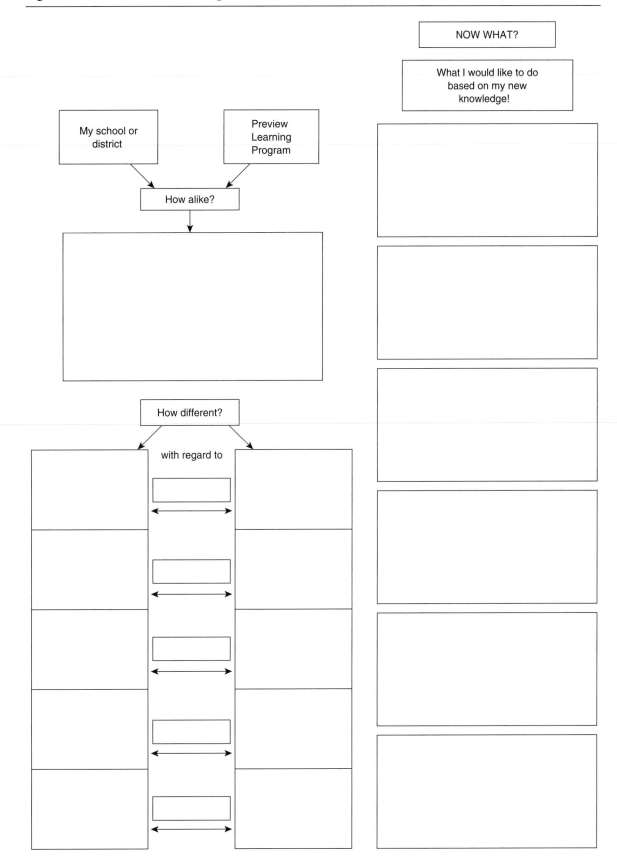

2. Review Chapter 6 to peruse the various professional growth designs for student learning that are incorporated there. Look for the day-to-day agendas for afternoon labs, and note the variety of learning opportunities for each educator. Study again Figure 6.6 to reexamine ways to embed staff development into the workday. Get a blank notebook; label it "Job-Embedded Staff Development in My School (use the actual name) or My District (use the actual name)." Have enough pages in the notebook to record your ongoing thoughts. Begin by listing at least five ways that you can begin to work within policy in your school or system to embed opportunities for student learning through staff development. Keep your personal antennae up for additional ways to expand your thinking, and record them in your notebook. This book, your work in progress, becomes your KnowBook. In other words, this is what you know to be true. These are your assumptions about what will work in your sphere of influence in the area of staff development. Make this the beginning of your directional plan for making a difference in the lives of students in the achievement gap.

Appendix A

Evaluation Results

PREVIEW LEARNING PROGRAM, YEAR ONE

Evaluation question one: To what extent did the PLP meet its overall goal of being a force for improved student learning and enhanced leadership and teaching practice?

Activity 1: Measure of fall performance

Type of method: Quantitative

Source of Information: Random sampling

Results: The record review of the end of unit reading test, given during the first six weeks of school to a random sampling of 563 students (PLP, N = 343; Control, N = 220) in grades 1–5 showed the PLP students with a mean score of 64.24 compared to the control group, with a 52.15 mean score. The standard deviation in the PLP group was 21.228, as opposed to 20.444 in the control group. The control group was made up of the students who qualified by virtue of their academic record to participate in the PLP, but for some reason were unable to participate.

The same information is shown in a breakdown by grades in Figure A.1.

A *t-test* of independent samples for equality of means is shown in Figure A.2 and a bar graph in Figure A.3. They illustrate the means at each grade level in both the control group and the PLP group of students.

Activity 2: Standardized test

Type of method: Quantitative

Source of information: Students enrolled in the Preview Learning Program

Results: PLP students increased standardized test performance by 5 normal curve equivalents (NCEs).

Figure A.1   Case Summaries

Group	Grade	N	Mean	Standard Deviation
Control	1	35	72.29	15.676
	2	44	65.34	17.307
	3	52	46.54	16.135
	4	51	42.67	17.448
	5	37	38.76	13.837
	Total	219	52.21	20.468
Preview Learning Program	1	64	83.22	13.751
	2	94	73.00	17.658
	3	75	55.53	17.774
	4	54	55.69	19.820
	5	56	47.77	15.901
	Total	343	64.24	21.228

Figure A.2   Independent Samples Test

	t-test for Equality of Means			95% Confidence Interval of the Difference	
	t	Sig. (two-tailed)	Mean Difference	Lower	Upper
Unit 1 Equal variances not assumed	6.745	.000	12.09	8.570	15.614

Activity 3: Survey of teacher use of reading strategies

Type of method: Quantitative

Source of information: Random sampling in the spring of the regular school year, following the first year's implementation of the PLP teachers who taught in the previous four-week summer program.

Results: Strategies "being used more frequently" to teach reading, as opposed to "using them the same" or "using them less frequently," include activating strategies, decoding thinking, graphic organizers, guided reading, and modeling. We know that all these strategies are effective in teaching the subject, and each

Figure A.3 Mean at Each Grade

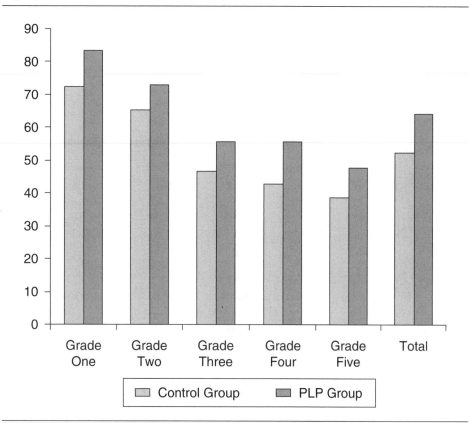

was described as being used less frequently in the regular classroom when the teachers started in the lab-based program.

Evaluation question two: Was the Preview Learning Program effective for students and teachers?

Activity 1: Reading pretest and posttest

Type of method: Quantitative

Source of information: Preview Learning Program students

Results: The bar graph in Figure A.4 shows the progress of the PLP students by grade level from the pretest to the posttest, and on to the unit one test in the fall of the regular school year.

Activity 2: Pretest and Posttest for Writing

Type of method: Quantitative

Source of information: Preview Learning Program students

Results: Ninety-four percent of the students maintained or gained on the writing assessment.

Figure A.4   Progress of PLP Students

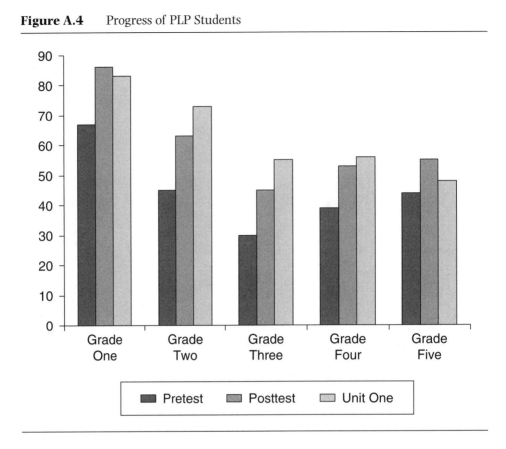

Activity 3: Student Attitude Survey

Type of method: Quantitative

Source of information: Students answered 11 questions regarding their attitudes or feelings about reading during the *first* and *last* week of the PLP. The survey is displayed in Chapter 7, in Figure 7.3.

Results: Significant positive changes in attitude were noted. The following items involved a *12 percent or greater positive change:*

• Reading is my favorite subject.	Item 1
• I want to become a better reader.	Item 6
• Reading will help me in life.	Item 8
• I learn about many things in reading.	Item 9
• Reading is easy for me.	Item 10

Activity 4: Educator Survey

Type of method: Quantitative

Source of information: Random sample of principals, feedback coaches, and grade-level teachers

Figure A.5   Mean at Each Grade

Mean = 4.7   Ranking 1(low) to 5 (high)   Pr = Principal; FBC = Feedback Coach;
T = Grade-Level Teacher

Survey Question	Pr	FBC	1T	2T	3T	4T	5T
1. I had the necessary resources to implement the PLP.	4.6	4.8	3.9	4.2	4.4	4.3	4.4
2. Scheduled meetings began and ended on time.	5.0	5.0	4.5	4.5	4.4	4.8	4.8
3. I was encouraged to try new strategies.	5.0	5.0	4.7	4.9	4.7	4.6	4.9
4. I had discussions with my feedback coach.	5.0	NA	4.5	4.8	4.8	4.5	4.9
5. The assistance of my coach was helpful in participating in the PLP.	5.0	NA	4.3	4.7	4.4	4.1	4.6
6. I had access to expertise of others when problems arose.	4.8	4.9	4.8	4.8	4.8	4.2	4.9
7. I had support available for implementing the new curriculum.	4.8	4.9	4.7	5.0	4.5	4.3	4.8
8. I developed better insights into students' unique learning needs.	4.8	5.0	4.6	4.7	4.6	4.5	4.7
9. I became open to new instructional strategies.	4.8	5.0	4.7	5.0	4.7	4.8	4.8
10. I engaged more regularly in discussions about teaching and learning needs.	4.8	5.0	4.7	4.5	4.4	4.6	4.3
11. I collaborated with my peers.	5.0	4.8	4.8	5.0	4.4	4.8	4.6
12. I had students who found the new curriculum appropriate to their instructional level.	4.8	4.6	4.3	4.2	4.4	4.0	4.4
13. My students were motivated to participate in daily activities.	4.8	4.9	4.7	4.8	4.5	4.2	4.7
Average	4.9	4.9	4.6	4.7	4.5	4.4	4.7

Results: Figure A.5 shows the list of survey questions and the responses from principals, feedback coaches, and teachers broken down by grade level. The scores are ranked on a scale of 1 (low) to 5 (high). The mean score is 4.7, indicating that the program was extremely successful. An individual analysis of each question will give guidance for future improvements. For example, question 12, on the appropriateness of the curriculum to the instructional level of the students, can be a source of dialogue before implementing the program again, even though the average score for the statement was 4.4. The score may mean that the teachers taught for mastery and not awareness; there is a need for more staff development in that particular area; the students' learning style did not align with the instructional strategies; or a number of other things. Because this score is the lowest of all the line item scores, it certainly bears thoughtful consideration.

Figures A.6a, A.6b, and A.6c continue the survey, but in this questionnaire the same group is asked to respond with a simple yes or no. The results strongly indicate that the teachers grew professionally in a standards-based way.

Figure A.6a Progress of PLP Students

Random Sample. N = Pr,5; FBC,11; 1T,15; 2T, 21; 3T,18; 4T,13; 5T,14

Pr = Principal; FBC = Feedback Coach;
T = Grade-Level Teacher

Survey Question: The Preview Learning Program has improved my ability to:	Pr Y	Pr N	FBC Y	FBC N	1T Y	1T N	2T Y	2T N	3T Y	3T N	4T Y	4T N	5T Y	5T N
• Focus on student learning	5		11		15		21		18		13		14	
• Understand the link between assessment and instruction	5		11		15		19	2	18		13		13	1
• Identify new ways to use curriculum	5		11		15		20	1	18		13		14	
• Explore new teaching strategies	5		11		15		21		18		13		14	
• Teach to an essential question	4	1	11		14	1	19	2	18		12	1	14	
• Have an understanding of how students develop and learn	5		10	1	14	1	20	1	16	2	11	2	11	3
• Know how to manage and monitor student learning	5		11		14	1	21		15	3	13		13	1
• Orchestrate learning in group settings	5		11		15		21		15	3	13		11	3
• Know how to place a premium on students' engagement	5		11		15		21		14	4	12	1	13	1
• Assess students' progress to enhance students' learning	5		11		15		21		15	3	13		14	
• Use a portfolio more effectively with students	5		11		14	1	21		18		13		13	1
• Have open communication and collaborative problem solving	5		11		15		21		13	5	11	2	13	1
• Understand that fully 95% of all children can be taught to read	5		11		14	1	19	2	15	3	12	1	11	3

160

Figure A.6b Educator Survey

Pr = Principal; FBC = Feedback Coach;
T = Grade-Level Teacher

Random Sample. N = Pr,5; FBC,11; 1T,15; 2T, 21; 3T,18; 4T,13; 5T,14

Survey Question: The Preview Learning Program has improved my ability to:	Pr Y	Pr N	FBC Y	FBC N	1T Y	1T N	2T Y	2T N	3T Y	3T N	4T Y	4T N	5T Y	5T N
• Directly teach decoding	5		9	2	15		20	1	16	2	12	1	8	6
• Directly teach comprehension	5		11		15		21		15	3	13		13	1
• Explicitly teach the process of writing	5		11		14	1	19	2	17	1	12	1	12	2
• Have vocabulary instruction that includes a variety of complementary methods	5		11		15		21		18		13		14	
• Use a structured design to develop a lesson	5		11		15		21		18		13		14	
• Explore how portfolio assessment can help both students and teachers track learning	5		11		15		21		18		13		14	
• Teach to a standard instructional level	5		11		15		20	1	18		12	1	14	

Figure A.6c Educator Professional Growth Survey Response Totals

Random Sample. N = Pr,5; FBC,11; 1T,15; 2T, 21; 3T,18; 4T,13; 5T,14

Pr = Principal; FBC = Feedback Coach;
T = Grade-Level Teacher

Survey Sentence Stem: In the Preview Learning Program:	Pr Y	Pr N	FBC Y	FBC N	1T Y	1T N	2T Y	2T N	3T Y	3T N	4T Y	4T N	5T Y	5T N
• A supportive climate of professional community was created.	5		11		15		21		18		13		13	1
• Opportunities to network and learn from colleagues were supported.	5		11		15		21		17	1	13		14	
• The opportunity to seek meaning and construct new knowledge in teaching was achieved for me.	5		11		15		21		18		13		14	
• The staff development that I participated in will improve my practice in my regular classroom.	5		11		15		20	1	18		13		14	
• Research was used to guide activities.	5		11		15		20	1	17	1	13		14	
• The link between research and improving teaching became clear to me.	5		10	1	14	1	21		18		12	1	13	1
• I learned to think systematically about my teaching.	5		11		15		21	1	18	1	13		13	1
• Thinking reflectively became part of my day.	5		11		15		20	1	17	1	13		14	

Evaluation question three: What components of the PLP were the most effective? What needs to be strengthened?

Activity 1: Teacher survey

Type of method: Quantitative and qualitative

Source of information: Random sampling of PLP principals, feedback coaches, and grade-level teachers

Results: Based on the analysis of the quantitative data in the above activity, the following program components received high marks across the board:

- Implementation of new teaching strategies
- Having feedback coaches
- Ability to collaborate
- Reflecting
- Linking instruction and assessment
- Using a focused curriculum
- Determining instructional strategies
- Engaging students
- Having student portfolios
- Using direct and explicit teaching
- Having content-specific staff development
- Developing a supportive climate.

Activity 2: Written Educator Survey

Type of method: Quantitative

Source of information: Random sampling of PLP principals, feedback coaches, and grade-level teachers. The respondents were asked to complete a sentence stem indicating the program element that was most helpful to them, and the element that was least helpful. Figure A.7 identifies the groups who responded, but does *not* indicate the numbers of people who made the response.

Results: See Figure A.7

Evaluation question 4: What reading content and related teaching strategies would you like to spend more time learning about in your staff development opportunities?

Activity: Survey

Type of method: Quantitative

Source of information: Random sampling of PLP principals, feedback coaches, and grade-level teachers. The information will be used as a needs assessment for future skill development, staff development opportunities.

Results: See Figure A.8

Figure A.7 Educator Survey Responses by Roles

Random Sample: N = 97

Pr = Principal; FBC = Feedback Coach; T = Grade-Level Teacher

Survey sentence stem*: The most helpful thing to me in the Preview Learning Program was	Pr	FBC	1T	2T	3T	4T	5T
• Supervisory support	x	x					
• Graphic organizers	x					x	x
• Running records	x	x	x	x	x	x	
• Prepared lesson plans	x						x
• Guided reading	x	x	x	x		x	x
• Curriculum	x		x	x	x		x
• Staff development	x	x		x	x	x	
• Collaborating	x	x	x	x			x
• The principal				x	x	x	
• The feedback coach				x		x	
• Small class size					x		
Survey sentence stem: The least helpful thing to me in the Preview Learning Program was							
• Emphasis on reflection	x		x		x	x	x
• Meeting time with other coaches		x					
• Having to scaffold lessons					x	x	
• Lack of planning time				x			

*Note: Responses were self-generated. If only one person in the sample responded by writing a topic, that topic is shown here with an X in the column. It is interesting to note that of the many components in the PLP, 11 were written in as being helpful to an individual in some way. The converse is true in the least helpful items, too.

Figure A.8 Needs Assessment: Skill Development Staff Development Opportunity

Random Sample: N = 97

Pr = Principal; FBC = Feedback Coach; T = Grade-Level Teacher

Survey Sentence Stem: I would like to spend more time learning about	Pr	FBC	1T	2T	3T	4T	5T
• Vocabulary building	x	x				x	
• The writing process	x	x	x	x	x	x	x
• Guided reading	x	x	x	x		x	x
• Running records	x	x	x	x		x	
• Teaching spelling effectively		x				x	x
• Assessment tools and strategies				x	x	x	x
• Differentiating reading instruction							x
• Graphic organizers		x		x	x	x	x
• Reading strategies			x	x	x	x	
• Forming flexible groups				x	x	x	x

Appendix B

Expanding the Concept

PREVIEW LEARNING PROGRAM

Figure B.1   Teaching an Essential Skill for Achievement for Low-Achieving Students

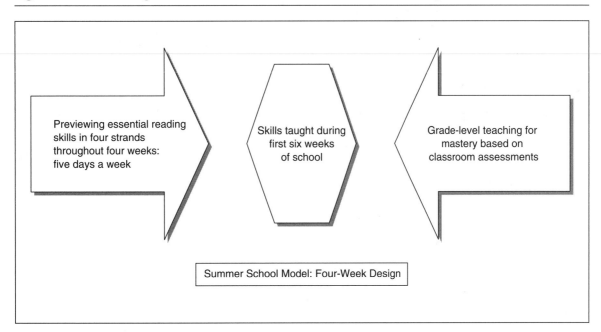

Previewing essential reading skills in four strands throughout four weeks: five days a week

Skills taught during first six weeks of school

Grade-level teaching for mastery based on classroom assessments

Summer School Model: Four-Week Design

Figure B.2   Summer School Model: Four-Week Design

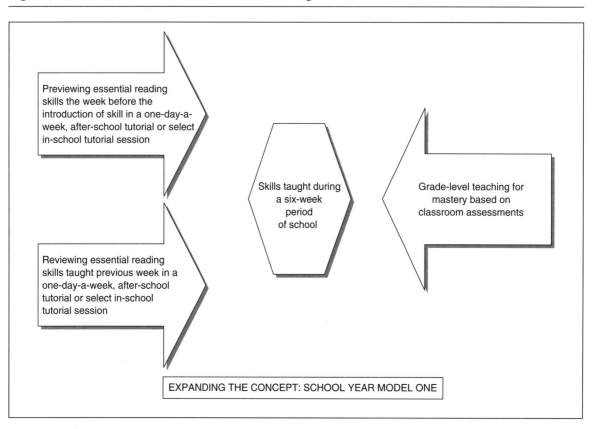

Figure B.3   School Year: Model Two

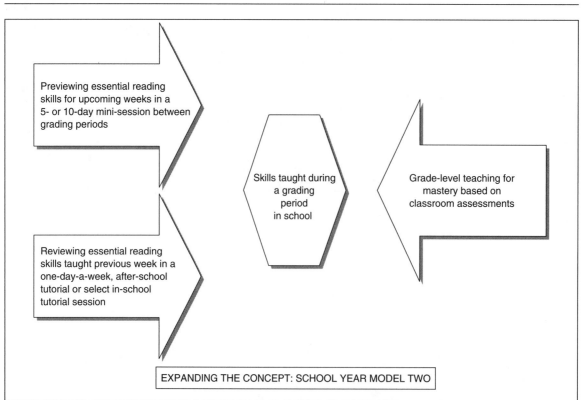

Glossary

SELECTED TERMS USED IN THE PREVIEW LEARNING PROGRAM

Acquisition lesson: A structured design to intentionally engage students in meaningful ways using Principles of Learning. *See Chapter 5.*

Bonelets: A graphic tool used to show building blocks within a category. In the PLP bonelets show subcategories in the Fishbone Model. *See Chapter 2.*

Compact skills or concepts: In a prioritized curriculum, they are "nice to know" understandings and "how-to" skills that add interest to the material. For the at-risk child, twenty percent of the time may be spent on compact skills or concepts. *See Chapters 4 and 5.*

Decoding: Strategies used to determine a new word such as visually scanning letter patterns or deliberately using a letter/sound mapping system. *See Chapter 5.*

Effective teacher: One who facilitates the value-added learning of concepts, facts, and skills to a prescribed level and consciously replicates the same performance with different individuals over time. *See Chapter 3.*

Essential question: One overarching, global question that drives all the sub-questions that will ultimately provide answers for the larger question. An EQ springs from the upper levels of Bloom's Taxonomy. *See Chapters 3, 4, and 5.*

Essential skills or concepts: In a prioritized curriculum, basic/indispensable skills or concepts that are required as building blocks for success at the next level of attainment. For the at-risk child sixty to seventy percent of the time should be spent previewing essential skills. *See Chapters 4 and 5.*

Fishbone Model: A cause-and-effect graphic organizer used to systematically display thinking and give increased understanding to each component. *See Chapter 2.*

Hiring IQ: A results-based strategy for educator selection. See Introduction and *Chapter 3.*

Horizontal thinking: Creative and non-sequential ideas that push thoughts in a totally new direction. *See Chapter 2.*

Important skills or concepts: In a prioritized curriculum, understandings and "how-to" skills that are worthy of note, but a de-emphasis in preview time will not immediately jeopardize the attainment level. For the at-risk child, thirty percent of the time may be spent on important skills or concepts. *See Chapters 4 and 5.*

KnowBook: A cognitive journal; an instructional tool where learners record what they "know." *See Chapter 5.*

Lab-based staff development: A structured model, made up of multiple staff development designs, which focuses on the act of teaching and learning through collaboration, feedback, and reflection. *See Chapter 6.*

Logic Model: A comprehensive planning model that helps systems know in advance if a design includes strategies to reach a goal and attain the desired results. *See Chapter 2.*

Phonemic awareness: A conscious understanding that spoken words are made up of individual sounds. *See Chapters 4 and 5.*

Phonics: The relationship between the sounds of words and their written systems. *See Chapters 4 and 5.*

Phonological awareness: Ability to break a spoken word into syllables, recognize and produce rhymes, and identify the number of words in a sentence. *See Chapters 4 and 5.*

Preview curriculum: A curriculum specifically designed to ensure learning for the low-achieving child with intelligence in the range of normal. *See Chapter 4.*

Preview learning lesson: Essential skills, facts, or concepts intentionally taught for awareness in advance of a teaching time for mastery. *See Chapter 4.*

Preview learning program: Teaching more, not less, to a targeted population; skill-based intervention; prioritized curriculum; lab-based staff development; instructional design; formative and summative assessment; and educator selection. *See Chapter 2.*

Prioritized curriculum: Grade and subject-specific objectives and skills designated as essential (top 50%) to master; important (30 percent); or compact (20 percent). *See Chapter 4.*

Scaffolding: An explicit strategy used to develop independence in the learner through planned support and subsequent withdrawal of strategies; effective in bridging the gap between abstract and concrete. *See Chapters 4 and 5.*

Touch points: Places where the teacher intentionally stops to check for understanding of the skill or concept to determine *what* the next learning should be and *how* to strategically present it. *See Chapters 4 and 5.*

Vertical thinking: Thoughts that are developmentally and sequentially organized to give a deeper understanding of something with which others have already had success. *See Chapter 2.*

Resources:
Planning Tools

Worksheet 1.1 My District

District Totals	Number	Percent
Number of Schools: Total		
• Elementary		
• Middle		
• Secondary		
• Special		
Grades Served		
Number of Students K–12		
• White		
• African American		
• Hispanic		
• Asian		
• Native American		
• Pacific Islander		
Economically Disadvantaged		

Worksheet 1.2

Nationally Normed Achievement Tests Used in My District	
Notes:	1.
	2.
	3.
	4.
	5.
	6.

Local Assessments Used in My District (i.e., districtwide tests)	
Notes:	1.
	2.
	3.
	4.
	5.
	6.

Worksheet 1.3   My District: Testing Data Measuring Student Academic Growth by Grade Level

Number of Students Tested in Reading	First Quartile	% of Total	Second Quartile	% of Total	Third Quartile	% of Total	Fourth Quartile	% of Total	Total
Grade 2									
Grade 3									
Grade 4									
Grade 5									

Worksheet 1.4   My District: Testing Data Measuring Student Academic Growth by Schools

Students First Quartile	%	# White	%	# African-American	%	# Hispanic	%	# Asian	%	# Native American	%	# Pacific Islanders	%
School 1													
School 2													
School 3													
School 4													
School 5													
School 6													
School 7													
School 8													
School 9													
School 10													
School 11													
School 12													
School 13													
School 14													
School 15													
School 16													
School 17													
School 18													
School 19													
School 20													
School 21													
School 22													
School 23													
School 24													
School 25													
School 26													
School 27													
School 28													
School 29													
School 30													

Worksheet 1.5   My District: Planning Team

District Administrators	Notes
1.	
2.	
3.	
4.	
5.	
School-Specific Educators	
1.	
2.	
3.	
4.	
5.	
Data Specialists	
1.	
2.	
3.	
4.	
5.	

Worksheet 1.6 My District

My Questions at This Point:
1.
2.
3.
4.
5.
6.
7.

Worksheet 1.7 My District: Prioritizing Next Steps

Priority Order	Item

Worksheet 2.1   Wisdom Storm (Vertical Thinking)

Things that I know about underachieving students include…

➢

➢

➢

➢

➢

➢

Worksheet 2.2   Synectics (Horizontal Thinking)

A low-achieving student is like _____

_____

_____

_____

_____

_____

_____

_____

_____

_____

because _____

_____

_____

_____

_____

_____

_____

_____

_____

_____

_____

_____

_____

_____

_____

Worksheet 2.3   Storytelling (Horizontal Thinking)

I. Once upon a time there was a group of students
  who did not achieve academically.

II. One day something spectacular happened for the students. The district

_____

_____

_____

_____

_____

_____

_____

_____

III. This is how it turned out. _____

_____

_____

_____

_____

_____

_____

_____

_____

_____

_____

_____

_____

_____

_____

_____

_____

Worksheet 2.4a   Powerful Questions: What-if Format

Domain	What-if Question
Standards	
Curriculum	

Worksheet 2.4b

Domain	What-if Question
Instruction	
Personnel	

Worksheet 2.4c

Domain	What-if Question
Personnel	
Professional Development	

Worksheet 2.4d

Domain	What-if Question
Assessment	
Evaluation	

Worksheet 2.4e

Domain	What-if Question
Administration	
Other	

Worksheet 2.5 My Planning Fishbone

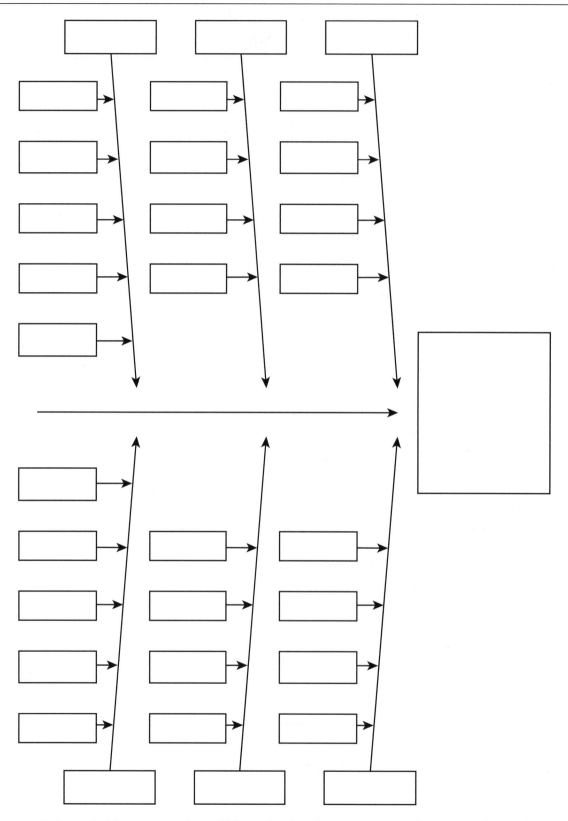

Worksheet 2.6 Planning Model for _____ District

Element	Description
Problem: Statement of Need	• • • •
Desired Results	• • • •
Review of Literature	
Planning and Implementation Strategies	• • • • •
Assumptions on Which to Base Innovation	• • • • • • • •
School and Community Resources	

Worksheet 4.1   Preview Learning: The Question Wheel in Chart Form

Overarching Question:

First Order Question	Second Order Question	Third Order Question	Fourth Order Question

Worksheet 4.2   Cluster Map: Essential Questions and Foundation Questions

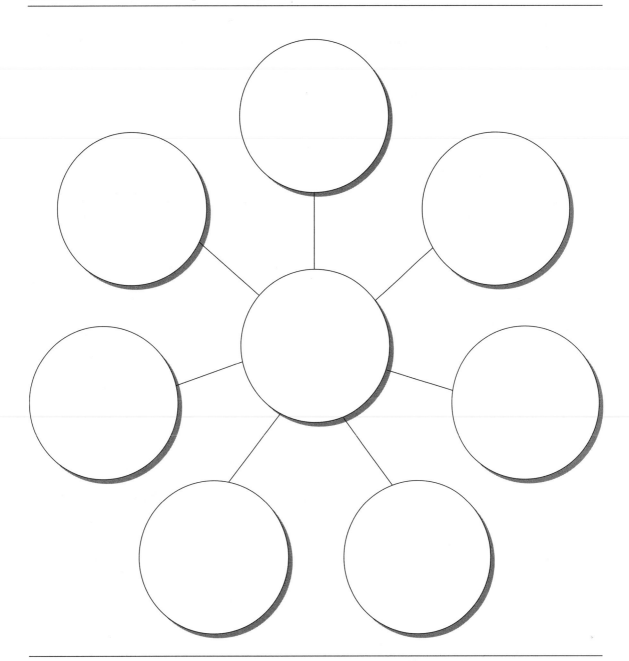

Worksheet 5.1   Critical Decision Map: "Seeing" My Thinking

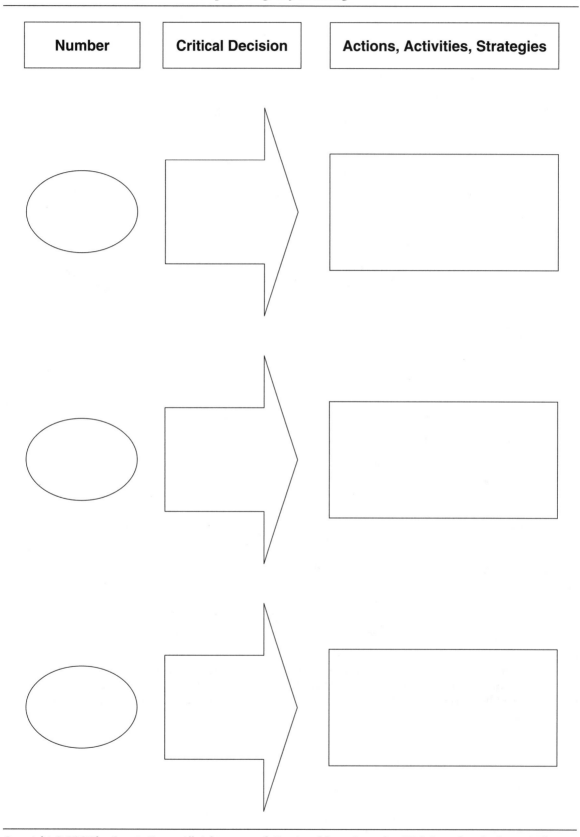

| Number | Critical Decision | Actions, Activities, Strategies |

Worksheet 5.2 Prioritized Skills and Concepts

Standards-based *Essential* Academic Skills (*E*) Grade Level:_____	Standards-based *Important* Academic Skills (*I*) Grade Level:_____	Standards-based *Compact* Academic Skills (*C*) Grade Level:_____
•	•	•
•	•	•
•	•	•
•	•	•
•	•	•
•	•	•
•	•	•
•	•	•
•	•	•
•	•	•
•	•	•
•	•	•
•	•	•
•	•	•
•	•	•

Worksheet 5.3 Literacy Instructional Framework Grade Four: Language Arts

Topic	Standard	Priority: E, I, or C
•		
•		
•		
•		
•		
•		
•		
•		
•		
•		
•		
•		
•		
•		
•		
•		
•		
•		
•		
•		
•		
•		
•		
•		
•		
•		

Worksheet 5.4   Literacy Instructional Framework for Acquisition Learning

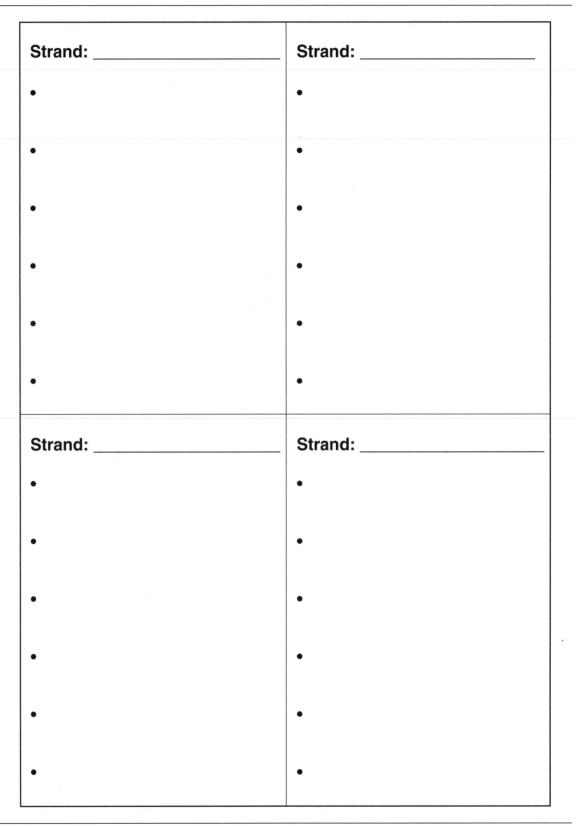

Strand: _____	Strand: _____
•	•
•	•
•	•
•	•
•	•
•	•

Strand: _____	Strand: _____
•	•
•	•
•	•
•	•
•	•

Worksheet 6.1 Preview Learning – Compare and Contrast

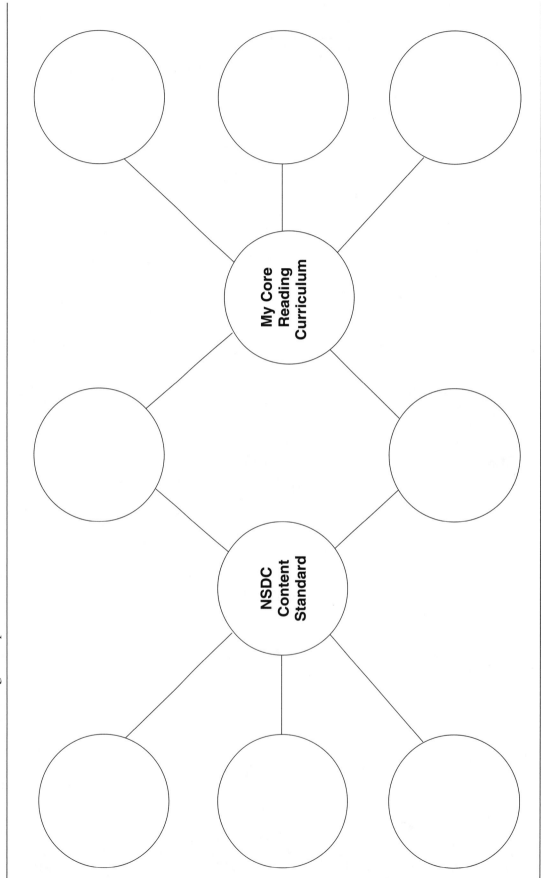

My Core Reading Curriculum

NSDC Content Standard

Worksheet 6.2   Preview Learning Staff Development Agenda for Teachers, Coaches, and Administrators

Site Code: 1 = Individual School
2 = Staff Development Center
3 = Individual Option

(Time)
(Week, Day)

Time	Staff Development Design	Topic	Site	Leader or Facilitator	Guiding Question	Follow-up Staff Development	Expected Outcome	Notes

Worksheet 6.3   Preview Learning Curriculum Feedback

Grade Level: _____ PLP Site: _____

Strengths of the Curriculum	"Not-yets" of the Curriculum
•	•
•	•
•	•
•	•
•	•
•	•
•	•
•	•
•	•
•	•
•	•
•	•

Worksheet 7.1   Evaluation Framework

Program Goal:

Measurable Objectives:

-
-
-
-

Information Needed and Timeline:

-
-
-
-
-

Data Sources:

-
-
-
-
-

Worksheet 7.2   Formative Assessment Index

Event	Formative Assessment
Curriculum development	• • •
Teacher, Administrator, Coach selection	• • •
Student selection	• • • • • •
Instructional design	• • •
Staff development	• • • • • • • •
Student and teacher learning	• • • • • • • •

Worksheet 7.3 Formative Assessment Rubric Level of Use

Level One	
Level Two	
Level Three	
Level Four	

Worksheet 7.4   Preview Learning Feedback Coach Basic Follow-up Questions

Worksheet 7.5   Purpose of Principal Walk-Through

The purpose of the principal walk-through in the PLP is:

-
-
-
-
-
-
-

Worksheet 7.6   Teaching Essential Skills for Achievement of Low-Achieving Students

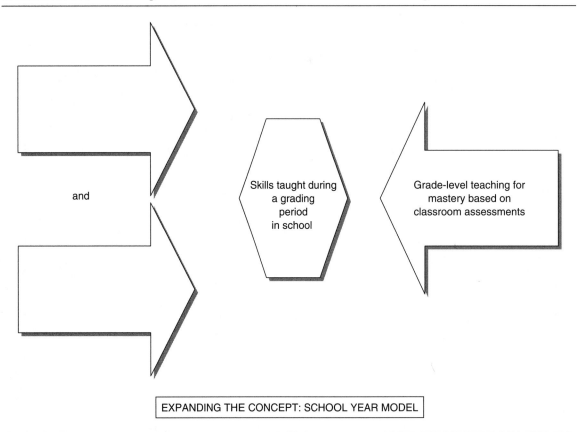

and

Skills taught during
a grading
period
in school

Grade-level teaching for
mastery based on
classroom assessments

EXPANDING THE CONCEPT: SCHOOL YEAR MODEL

References

Abernathy, R., & Reardon, M. (2003). *Hot tips for facilitators: Strategies to make life easier for anyone who leads, guides, teaches, or trains groups.* Tucson: Zephyr.

Ainsworth, L. (2003). *"Unwrapping" the standards: A simple process to make standards manageable.* Denver: Advanced Learning Press.

Allen, R. (2003, December). An early taste of college: Accelerated learning with support motivates urban students. *Education Update, 45*(8), 1, 3, 8.

Allington, R. L. (2002, June). *The six Ts of effective elementary literacy instruction.* Originally published in *Phi Delta Kappan* as "What I've learned about effective reading instruction from a decade of studying exemplary elementary classroom teachers." Retrieved November 20, 2005 from www.readingrockets.org/article.pphp?ID=413

Allington, R. L., & Cunningham, P. M. (1996). *Schools that work: Where all children read and write.* New York: HarperCollins.

Allington, R. L., & Johnston, P. H. (2001). What do we know about effective fourth grade teachers and their classrooms? In: C. Roller (Ed.), *Learning to teach reading: Setting the research agenda* (pp. 150–165). Newark, DE: International Reading Association.

Amrein, A. L., & Berliner, D. C. (2002). High-stakes testing, uncertainty, and student learning. *Educational Policy Analysis Archives, 10*(18), 70. Retrieved September 13, 2004 from http://epaa.asu.edu/epaa/v10n18

Armstrong, T. (1998). *Awakening genius in the classroom.* Alexandria, VA: Association for Supervision and Curriculum Development.

Arter, J., & McTighe, J. (2001). Scoring rubrics in the classroom: Using performance for assessing and improving student performance. In T. R. Guskey & R. J. Marzano (Series Eds.), *Experts in assessment.* Thousand Oaks, CA: Corwin Press.

Astuto, T., Clark, D. L., Read, A., McGree, K., & Fernandez, L. P. (1993). *Challenges to dominant assumptions controlling educational reform.* Andover, ME: The Regional Laboratory for Educational Improvement of the Northeast and Islands.

Audet, R. H., & Jordan, L. K. (2003). *Standards in the classroom: An implementation guide for teachers of science and mathematics.* Thousand Oaks, CA: Corwin Press.

Barth, P., Haycock, K., Jackson, H., Mora, K., Ruiz, P., Robinson, S., & Wilkins, A. (Eds.). (1999). *Dispelling the myth: High-poverty schools exceeding expectations.* Washington, DC: Education Trust in Cooperation with the Council of Chief State School Officers and partially funded by the U.S. Department of Education.

Beane, J. (Ed.). (1995). *Toward a coherent curriculum.* Alexandria, VA: Association for Supervision and Curriculum Development.

Beck, I. L. (1986, April). Using Research on Reading. *Educational Leadership, 43*(7), 13–15.

Bella, N. J. (2004). *Reflective analysis of student work: Improving teaching through collaboration.* Thousand Oaks, CA: Corwin Press.

Bender, W. N., & Larkin, M. J. (2003). *Reading strategies for elementary students with learning difficulties.* Thousand Oaks, CA: Corwin Press.

Bernhardt, V. L. (1999, June). *Databases can help teachers with standards implementation* (Monograph No. 5.). Los Osos, CA: California Association for Supervision and Curriculum Development.

Bernhardt, V. L. (2003a). No schools left behind. *Educational Leadership, 60*(5), 26–30.

Bernhardt, V. L. (2003b). *Using data to improve student learning in elementary school.* Larchmont, NY: Eye on Education.

Bernhardt, V. L., von Blanckensee, L., Lauck, M., Rebello, F., Bonilla, G., & Tribbey, M. (2000). *The example school portfolio, a companion to the school portfolio: A comprehensive framework for school improvement.* Larchmont, NY: Eye on Education.

Billmeyer, R., & Barton, M. L. (1998). *Teaching reading in the content area: If not me, then who?* (Blackline masters). Aurora, CO: Mid-continent Regional Educational Laboratory.

Black, P., & William, D. (1998). Assessment and classroom learning. *Educational assessment: Principles, policy, and practice, 5*(1), 7–74. Also summarized in Black and William (1998), Inside the black box: Raising standards through classroom assessment, *Phi Delta Kappan, 80*(2), 139–148.

Blanchard, K., & Waghorn, T. (1997). *Mission possible.* New York: McGraw-Hill.

Bloom, B. (1954). *Taxonomy of educational objectives handbook I: Cognitive domain.* New York: McKay.

Bloom, B. (1984). The search for methods of group instruction as effective as one-to-one tutoring. *Educational Leadership, 41*(8), 4–17.

Boston, C. (2002). The concept of formative assessment. *Practical Assessment, Research & Evaluation, 8*(9). Retrieved June 12, 2004 from http://PAREonline.net/getun .asp?v =8+n=9

Boyles, C. B. (2005). *Scaffolding grade-level learning for at-risk and exceptional students.* Boone, NC: Learning-Focused Solutions.

Bracey, G. W. (2002). International comparison: An excuse to avoid meaningful educational reform. *Education Week, 21*(19), 30–32.

Brophy, J. E., & Evertson, C. (1977). Teacher behaviors and student learning in second and third grades. In G. D. Borich (Ed.), *The appraisal of teaching: Concepts and process* (pp. 79–95). Reading, MA: Addison-Wesley.

Brozo, W. G., & Hargis, C. (2003, November). Using low-stakes reading assessment. *Educational Leadership, 61*(3), 60–64.

Buckingham, M., & Clifton, D. O. (2001). *Now, discover your strengths.* New York: The Free Press.

Burkhardt, G. (2002, December). A closer look at the minority achievement gap. *ERS Spectrum, 19*(2), 4–10.

Caine, R. N., & Caine, G. (1997). *Education on the edge of possibility.* Alexandria, VA: Association for Supervision and Curriculum Development.

Calhoun, E. (2004). *Using data to assess our reading program.* Alexandria, VA: Association for Supervision and Curriculum Development.

Carbo, M., Dunn, R., & Dunn, K. (1986). *Teaching students to read through their individual learning styles.* Englewood Cliffs, NJ: Prentice Hall.

Carr, J. F., & Harris, D. E. (2001). *Succeeding with standards: Linking curriculum, assessment, and action planning.* Alexandria, VA: Association for Supervision and Curriculum Development.

Cawelti, G. (Ed.). (1999). *Handbook of research on improving student achievement* (2nd ed.). Arlington, VA: Educational Testing Service.

Chapman, C. (1993). *If the shoe fits: How to develop multiple intelligences in the classroom.* Thousand Oaks, CA: Corwin Press.

Chapman, C., & Freeman, L. (1996). *Multiple intelligences: Centers and projects.* Thousand Oaks, CA: Corwin Press.

Chapman, C., & King, R. (2003a). *Differentiated instructional strategies for reading in the content area.* Thousand Oaks, CA: Corwin Press.

Chapman, C., & King, R. (2003b). *Differentiated instructional strategies for writing in the content area.* Thousand Oaks, CA: Corwin Press.

Chapman, C., & King, R. (2005). *Differentiated assessment strategies: One tool doesn't fit all.* Thousand Oaks, CA: Corwin Press.

Collins, J. (2001). *Good to great.* New York: HarperCollins.

Commission on Reading. (1985). *Becoming a nation of readers.* Washington, DC: National Academy of Education & the Center for the Study of Reading.

Corcoran, T., Fuhrman, S. H., & Belcher, C. L. (2001). The district role in instructional improvement. *Phi Delta Kappan, 83*(1), 78–84.

Costa, A. L., & Garmston, R. J. (1990). *The art of cognitive coaching: Supervision for intelligent teaching.* Sacramento, CA: Institute for Intelligent Behavior.

Costa, A. L., & Garmston, R. J. (1996). *Cognitive coaching: A foundation for renaissance schools.* Berkeley, CA: Institute for Intelligent Behavior.

Cotton, K. (1999). *Research you can use to improve results.* Portland, OR: Northwest Regional Educational Laboratory and Association for Supervision and Curriculum Development.

Creighton, T. B. (2001). *Schools and data: The educator's guide for using data to improve decision making.* Thousand Oaks, CA: Corwin Press.

Csikszentmihalyi, M. (1991). *Flow.* New York: Harper Perennial.

Danielson, C. (1996). *Enhancing professional practice: A framework for teaching.* Alexandria, VA: Association for Supervision and Curriculum Development.

Danielson, C., & Abrutyn, L. (1997). *An introduction to using portfolios in the classroom.* Alexandria, VA: Association for Supervision and Curriculum Development.

Darling-Hammond, L. (1997). *The right to learn.* San Francisco: Jossey-Bass.

Darling-Hammond, L. (1999). *Teacher quality and student achievement: A review of state policy evidence.* Seattle: Center for Teaching Policy, University of Washington.

DeBono, E. (1970). *Lateral thinking.* New York: Harper & Row.

DeBono, E. (1985). *Six thinking hats.* New York: Little, Brown.

Denton, D. R. (2002). *Summer school: Unfulfilled promise* (report). Atlanta: Southern Regional Education Board. Retrieved September 14, 2004 from www.sreb.org/programs/srr/pub/Summer_School.pdf

Downey, C. J., Steffy, B. E., English, F. W., Frase, L. E., & Poston, W. K., Jr. (2004). *The three-minute classroom walk-through: Changing school supervisory practice one teacher at a time.* Thousand Oaks, CA: Corwin Press.

Drucker, P. (2005). *Conservation Forum Quotations Peter Drucker 1909-* .www.conservativeforum.org/authquot.asp?ID=229

Duffy, G. G. (1997). Powerful models or powerful teachers? An argument for teachers-as-entrepreneur. In S. Stahl & O. Hayes (Eds.), *Instructional models in reading* (pp. 351–365). Mahwah, NJ: Erlbaum.

Dundon, E. (2005). Innovation triangle. *Leadership Excellence, 22*(3), 15.

Easton, L. B. (Ed.). (2004). *Powerful designs for professional learning.* Oxford, OH: National Staff Development Council.

Edmonds, R. (1979). Effective schools for the urban poor. *Educational Leadership, 37*(1), 15–24.

Educational Research Service. (2001). *What can schools do to reduce the achievement gap?* (ERS on the Same Page Series). Arlington, VA: Author. Retrieved April 12, 2005 from www.ers.org/otsp/otsp3.htm

Eisner, E. W. (2003 December/2004 January). Preparing for today and tomorrow. *Educational Leadership, 61*(4), 6–10.

Elmore, R. F. (2003, November). A plea for strong practice. *Educational Leadership, 61*(3), 10.

English, F. W. (2000). *Deciding what to teach and test: Developing, aligning, and auditing the curriculum.* Thousand Oaks, CA: Corwin Press.

Erickson, H. L. (1998). *Concept-based curriculum and instruction: Teaching beyond the facts.* Thousand Oaks, CA: Corwin Press.

Ferguson, R. F. (2002). Addressing racial disparities in high-achieving suburban schools. North Central Regional Educational Laboratory. *Policy Issues, 13*(12).

Fitzharris, L. H. (2005, Winter). Making all the right connections: Curriculum design helps teachers see the bigger picture that students experience, then see logical connections. *Journal of Staff Development, 26*(1), 24–28.

Fitzpatrick, K. A. (1997). *Indicators of schools of quality: Schoolwide indicators of quality* (Vol. 1). Schaumburg, IL: National Study of School Evaluation.

Fletcher, J. M., & Lyon, G. R. (1998). Reading: A research-based approach. In W. Evers (Ed.), *What's gone wrong in America's classrooms* (pp. 49–90). Stanford, CA: Hoover Institution Press.

Frey, C. (2003). Retrieved March 12, 2005 from www.innovationtools.com/Articles/ArticleDetails.asp?a=73

Fullan, M. (1993). *Change forces.* New York: Falmer Press.

Fullan, M. (1999). *Change forces: The sequel.* New York: Falmer Press.

Fullan, M. (2000). The three stories of education reform. *Phi Delta Kappan, 81*(8), 581–584.

Fullan, M. (2001). *The new meaning of educational change* (3rd ed.). New York: Teachers College Press.

Fullan, M. (2002). *Changing forces with a vengeance.* New York: RoutledgeFalmer.

Fullan, M. (2004, December 6). *Leadership and sustainability: Developing systems-thinkers-in-action.* (Keynote address at the National Staff Development Conference, Vancouver, British Columbia).

Fullan, M. G., & Miles, M. B. (1992). Getting reform right: What works and what doesn't. *Phi Delta Kappan, 73*(10), 745–752.

Gaddy, B., Dean, C. B., & Kendall, J. S. (2002). Creating standards-based learning experiences. In *Noteworthy perspective: Keeping the focus on learning* (pp. 11–24). Aurora, CO: Mid-continent Research for Education and Learning.

Gamoran, A. (1992). Access to excellence: Assignment to honors English in the transition from middle to high school. *Education Evaluation & Policy Analysis, 14*(3), 185–204.

Gardner, H. (1983). *Frames of mind: The theory of multiple intelligences.* New York: Basic Books.

Garmston, R., & Wellman, B. (1997). *The adaptive school: Leading and facilitating collaborative groups.* El Dorado Hills, CA: Four Hats Press.

Garmston, R., & Wellman, B. (2000). *The adaptive school: Developing and facilitating collaborative groups.* Norwood, MA: Christopher-Gordon.

Ginsberg, M. B. (2004). *Motivation matters: A workbook for school change.* San Francisco: Jossey-Bass.

Glanz, J. (2004). *The assistant principal's handbook: Strategies for success.* Thousand Oaks, CA: Corwin Press.

Glasgow, N. A., & Hicks, C. D. (2003). *What successful teachers do: 91 research-based classroom strategies for new and veteran teachers.* Thousand Oaks, CA: Corwin Press.

Glatthorn, A. A., & Fontana, J. (Eds.). (2000). *Coping with standards, tests, and accountability: Voices from the classroom.* Washington, DC: National Education Association.

Good, T. L., & Brophy, J. E. (1986). Teacher behavior and student achievement. In M. C. Wittrock (Ed.), *Handbook of research on teaching* (3rd ed.) (pp. 328–377). New York: Macmillan.

Gregory, G. H., & Chapman, C. (2002). *Differentiated instructional strategies: One size doesn't fit all.* Thousand Oaks, CA: Corwin Press.

Gregory, G. H., & Kuzmich, L. (2004). *Data-driven differentiation in the standards-based classroom.* Thousand Oaks, CA: Corwin Press.

Guskey, T. R. (1996, October 23). To transmit or to "construct"? The lure of trend infatuation in teacher professional development (Commentary). *Education Week, 16*(8), 34.

Guskey, T. R. (1996). Moving from means to ends. *Journal of Staff Development, 20*(2), 48.

Guskey, T. (2000). *Evaluating professional development.* Thousand Oaks, CA: Corwin Press.

Guskey, T. R. (2001, Summer). The backward approach. *Journal of Staff Development, 22*(3), 60.

Guskey, T. R. (2005a, Winter). Five key concepts kick off the process: Professional development provides the power to implement standards. *Journal of Staff Development, 26*(1), 36–40.

Guskey, T. R. (2005b, Winter). Taking a second look at accountability: Strong evidence reflecting the benefits of professional development is more important than ever before. *Journal of Staff Development, 26*(1), 10–17.

Guskey, T. R., & Bailey, J. M. (2001). Developing grading and reporting systems for student learning. In T. R. Guskey & R. J. Marzano (Series Eds.), *Experts in assessment.* Thousand Oaks, CA: Corwin Press.

Haberman, M. (1991). The pedagogy of poverty versus good teaching. *Phi Delta Kappan, 73*(4), 290–294.

Hannaford, C. (1995). *Smart moves: Why learning is not all in your head.* Arlington, VA: Great Ocean.

Harwell-Kee, K. (1999). Coaching. *Journal of Staff Development, 20*(3), 19–28.

Hassel, E. (1999). *Learning from the best: A toolkit for schools and districts based on the national awards program for model professional development.* Oak Brook, IL: North Central Regional Educational Laboratory.

Havner, V. (2005). Retrieved May 20, 2006 from http://www.the7thfire.com/NetworkMarketing.htm

Haycock, K. (1999). *Results: Good teaching matters.* Oxford, OH: National Staff Development Council.

Haycock, K. (2001a). Closing the achievement gap. *Educational Leadership, 58*(6), 6–11.

Haycock, K. (2001b). New frontiers for a new century: A national overview. *Thinking K–16, 5*(2), 1–2.

Haycock, K., Jerald, C., & Huang, S. (2001). Closing the gap: Done in a decade. *Thinking K–16, 5*(2), 3–21.

Hirsch, E. D., Jr. (1987). *Cultural literacy: What every American needs to know.* Boston: Houghton Mifflin.

Hirsch, E. D., Jr. (Ed). (1989). *A first dictionary of cultural literacy.* Boston: Houghton Mifflin.

Hirsch, E. D., Jr. (1996). *The schools we need: And why we don't have them.* New York: Doubleday.

Hirsh, S. (2005, Winter). Professional development and closing the achievement gap. *Theory into Practice, 44*(1), 38–44.

Holcomb, E. L. (2001). *Asking the right questions: Techniques for collaboration and school change.* Thousand Oaks, CA: Corwin Press.

Holloway, J. H. (2003, November). Linking professional development to student learning. *Educational Leadership, 61*(3), 85–87.

Honig, B. (2001). *Teaching our children to read: The components of an effective, comprehensive reading program.* Thousand Oaks, CA: Corwin Press.

Hunter, R. (2004). *Madeline Hunter's mastery teaching: Increasing instructional effectiveness in elementary and secondary schools* (updated edition). Thousand Oaks, CA: Corwin Press.

Husby, V. R. (2005). *Individualizing professional development: A framework for meeting school and district goals.* Thousand Oaks, CA: Corwin Press.

Hyerle, D. (1996). *Visual tools for constructing knowledge.* Alexandria, VA: Association for Supervision and Curriculum Development.

Hyerle, D. (Ed.). (2004). *Student successes with thinking maps: School-based research, results, and models for achievement using visual tools.* Thousand Oaks, CA: Corwin Press.

Innovation Network, Inc. (2005). *Logic model workbook.* Washington, DC: Author. Retrieved October 25, 2005 from www.innonet.org

Jacobs, H. H. (1997). *Mapping the big picture: Integrating curriculum and assessment K–12.* Alexandria, VA: Association for Supervision and Curriculum Development.

Johnston, R. C. (2001). Central office is critical bridge to help schools. *Education Week, 20*(25), 1, 18–19.

Johnson, R. S. (2002). *Using data to close the achievement gap: How to measure equity in our schools.* Thousand Oaks, CA: Corwin Press.

Kaggan, S. S. (2004). *30 reflective staff development exercises for educators.* Thousand Oaks, CA: Corwin Press.

Kaufman, R., & Herman, J. (1991). *Strategic planning in education.* Lancaster, PA: Technomic.

Killion, J. (2002). *Assessing impact: Evaluating staff development.* Oxford, OH: National Staff Development Council.

Killion, J. (2003). *Training manual for assessing impact: Evaluating staff development.* Oxford, OH: National Staff Development Council.

Killion, J. (2004). Journaling. In L. B. Easton (Ed.), *Powerful designs for professional learning* (pp. 127–133). Oxford, OH: National Staff Development Council.

Knight, J. (2004, Spring). Instructional coaches make progress through partnership: Intensive support can improve teaching. *Journal of Staff Development, 25*(2), 32–37.

Kober, N. (2001). It takes more than testing: Closing the achievement gap. Center on Education Policy. Retrieved July 21, 2005 from www.ctredpol.org/improving publicschools/closingachievementgap.pdf

Kotter, J. (1996). *Leading change.* Boston: Harvard Business School Press.

Kotulak, R. (1996). *Inside the brain: Revolutionary discoveries of how the mind works.* Kansas City, KS: Andrews McMeel Publishing.

Kouzes, J. M., & Posner, B. Z. (1993). *Credibility: How leaders gain and lose it, why people demand it.* San Francisco: Jossey-Bass.

Kouzes J. M., & Posner, B. Z. (2002). *The leadership challenge: How to keep getting extraordinary things done in organizations* (2nd ed.). San Francisco: Jossey-Bass.

Lambert, L. (2003). *Leadership capacity for lasting school improvement.* Alexandria, VA: Association for Supervision and Curriculum Development.

Larkin, M. J. (2001). Providing support for student independence through scaffolded instruction. *Teaching Exceptional Children, 34*(1), 30–35.

Lazear, D. (1998). *The rubrics way: Using MI to assess understanding.* Tucson: Zephyr.

Linn, R. (2000). Assessments and accountability. *Educational Researcher, 29*(2), 4–14.

Lipton, L., & Wellman, B. (2003). *Mentoring matters: A practical guide to learning-focused relationships* (2nd ed.). Sherman, CT: Mira Via.

Little, J. W. (1990). The persistence of privacy: The autonomy and initiative in teachers' professional relations. *Teachers College Board, 91*(4), 509–536.

Loucks-Horsley, S., Hewson, P., Love, N., & Stiles, K. E. (1998). *Designing professional development for teachers of science and mathematics.* Thousand Oaks, CA: Corwin Press.

March, J. K., & Peters, K. H. (2002, January). Curriculum development and instructional design in the effective schools process. *Phi Delta Kappan, 83*(5), 379–381.

Marzano, R. J. (2003). *What works in the classroom: Translating research into action.* Alexandria, VA: Association for Supervision and Curriculum Development.

Marzano, R. J. (2004). *Building background knowledge for academic achievement: Research on what works in schools.* Alexandria, VA: Association for Supervision and Curriculum Development.

Marzano, R. J., Pickering, D., & Pollock, J. E. (1993). *Assess student outcomes: Performance assessment using dimensions of learning model.* Alexandria, VA: Association for Supervision and Curriculum Development.

Marzano, R., & Pickering, D. (1997). *Dimensions of learning: Teacher's manual.* Alexandria, VA: Association for Supervision and Curriculum Development and Mid-continent Regional Educational Laboratory.

Marzano, R. J., Norford, J. S., Paynter, D. E., Pickering, D. J., & Gaddy, B. B. (2001). *A handbook for classroom instruction that works.* Alexandria, VA: Association for Supervision and Curriculum Development.

Marzano, R. J., Pickering, D. J., & Pollock, J. E. (2001). *Classroom instruction that works: Research-based strategies for increasing student achievement.* Alexandria, VA: Association for Supervision and Curriculum Development.

McEwan, E. K. (1998). *The principal's guide to raising reading achievement.* Thousand Oaks, CA: Corwin Press.

McEwan, E. K. (2002). *The ten traits of highly effective teachers.* Thousand Oaks, CA: Corwin Press.

McEwan, E. K. (2003). *The ten traits of highly effective principals: From good to great performance.* Thousand Oaks, CA: Corwin Press.

McEwan, E. K. (2004). *Seven strategies of highly effective readers: Using cognitive research to boost K–8 achievement.* Thousand Oaks, CA: Corwin Press.

McMillan, J. H. (2001). Essential assessment concepts for teachers and administrators. In T. R. Guskey & R. J. Marzano (Series Eds.), *Experts in assessment.* Thousand Oaks, CA: Corwin Press.

McTighe, J., & Wiggins, G. (1999). *The understanding by design handbook.* Alexandria, VA: Association for Supervision and Curriculum Development.

Meisels, S., Atkins-Burnett, S., Xue, Y., & Bickel, D. D. (2003). Creating a system of accountability: The impact of instructional assessment on elementary children's achievement scores. *Educational Policy Analysis Archives, 11*(9), 19pp. Retrieved August 15, 2004 from htpp://epaa.asu.edu/epaa/v11n9

Mizell, H. (2001, Summer). How to get there from here. *Journal of Staff Development, 22*(3), 18–20.

Moats, L. C. (1997). *A blueprint for professional development of teachers of early reading instruction.* Sacramento, CA: California State Board of Education, Comprehensive Reading Leadership Program.

Moats, L. C. (1999, June). Teaching reading *is* rocket science. In L. C. Moats (Ed.), *Commissioned Works of the National Institute of Child Health and Human Development*

(NICHD) Early Intervention Project (Item No. 372). Washington, DC: American Federation of Teachers.

Moats, L. C. (2000). *Every child reading: A professional development guide.* Washington, DC: The Learning First Alliance.

Murphy, C. (1997). Finding time for faculties to study together. *Journal of Staff Development, 18*(3), 29–32.

Murphy, C., & Lick, D. W. (1998). *Whole faculty study groups: A powerful way to change schools and enhance learning* (p. 4). Thousand Oaks, CA: Corwin Press.

Murphy, C., & Murphy, M. (2004). In L. B. Easton (Ed.), *Powerful designs for professional learning* (p. 218). Oxford, OH: National Staff Development Council.

National Board for Professional Teaching Standards. (1989). *What teachers should know and be able to do: The five core propositions of the national board.* Arlington, VA: Author. Retrieved October 15, 2005 from www.nbpts.org/about/coreprops.cfm

National Commission on Teaching and America's Future. (1996). *Doing what matters most: Teaching for America's future.* New York: Author.

National Commission on Teaching and America's Future. (1997). *Doing what matters most: Investing in quality teaching.* New York: Author.

National Staff Development Council. (1995). *Standards for staff development: Elementary school edition.* Oxford, OH: Author.

National Staff Development Council. (2001). *Standards for staff development* (revised). Oxford, OH: Author.

Nicholson, T. (1997). Closing the gap on reading failure: Social background, phonemic awareness, and learning to read. In B. A. Blachman (Ed.), *Foundations of reading acquisition and dyslexia* (pp. 381–407). Mahwah, NJ: Lawrence Erlbaum.

Olatokunbo, S. F. (2002). *Building effective afterschool programs.* Thousand Oaks, CA: Corwin Press.

Palus, C. J., & Horth, D. M. (2002). *The leader's edge.* San Francisco: Jossey-Bass.

Peterson, D., & VanDerWege, C. (2002, February). Guiding children to be strategic readers. *Phi Delta Kappan, 83*(6), 437–439.

Peterson, K. D., & Deal, T. E. (1998). How leaders influence the culture of schools. *Educational Leadership, 56*(1), 28–30.

Poglinco, S., Bach, A., Hovde, K., Rosenblum, S., Saunders, M., & Supovitz, J. (2003, May). *The heart of the matter: The coaching model in America's choice schools.* Philadelphia: Consortium for Policy Research in Education, University of Pennsylvania. Retrieved July 14, 2005 from www.cpre.org/Publications/ Publications_Research.htm

Poglinco, S., & Bach, A. (2004, January). The heart of the matter: Coaching as a vehicle for professional development. *Phi Delta Kappan, 85*(5), 398–400.

Psencik, K., & Hirsh, S. (2004). *Transforming schools through powerful planning.* Oxford, OH: National Staff Development Council.

Raider-Roth, M. (2005). *Trusting what you know: The high stakes of classroom relationships.* San Francisco: Jossey-Bass.

Reddell, P. (2004, Spring). Coaching can benefit students who have a higher hill to climb. *Journal of Staff Development, 25*(2), 20–26.

Reeves, D. B. (2001). *Performance assessment series: Elementary school edition.* Denver: Advanced Learning Press.

Reeves, D. B. (2002). *The leader's guide to standards: A blueprint for educational equity and excellence.* San Francisco: Jossey-Bass.

Reeves, D. B. (2004a). *Accountability in action: A blueprint for learning organizations* (2nd ed.). Denver: Advanced Learning Press.

Reeves, D. B. (2004b). *Assessing educational leaders: Evaluating performance for improved individual and organizational results.* Thousand Oaks, CA: Corwin Press and National Association of Secondary School Principals.

Rettig, M. D., McCullough, L. L., Santos, K., & Watson, C. K. (2003, November). A blueprint for increasing student achievement. *Educational Leadership, 61*(3), 71–76.

Rettig, M. D., McCullough, L. L., Santos, K. E., & Watson, C. K. (2004). *From rigorous standards to student achievement: A practical process.* Larchmont, NY: Eye on Education.

Rice, J. K. (2003). *Teacher quality: Understanding the effectiveness of teacher attributes.* Washington, DC: Economic Policy Institute.

Richardson, J. (2002, April). Reshaping schools from the top down. *Results,* April 2002.

Richardson, J. & Hirsch, S. (Eds.). (2001). *Tools for growing the NSDC standards.* Oxford, OH: National Staff Development Council.

Robbins, P. (1991). *How to plan and implement a peer coaching program.* Alexandria, VA: Association for Supervision and Curriculum Development.

Robbins, P. (2004). Peer coaching. In L. B. Easton (Ed.), *Powerful designs for professional learning* (pp. 163–174). Oxford, OH: National Staff Development Council.

Robbins, P., & Alvy, H. B. (2003). *The principal's companion: Strategies and hints to make the job easier* (2nd ed.). Thousand Oaks, CA: Corwin Press.

Rodriguez, M. C. (2004). The role of classroom assessment in student performance on TIMSS. *Applied Measurement in Education, 17*(1), 1–24.

Roy, P. (2005, February). A fresh look at follow-up. *Results,* February 2005.

Roy, P., & Hord, S. (2003). *Moving NSDC's staff development standards into practice: Innovation configurations.* Oxford, OH: National Staff Development Council.

Sanders, J. R. (2000). *Evaluating school programs: An educator's guide.* Thousand Oaks, CA: Corwin Press.

Sanders, W. L. (1998, December). Value-added assessment. *School Administrator, 55,* 101–113.

Sanders, W., & Rivers, J. C. (1996). *Cumulative and residual effects of teachers on future student academic achievement.* Knoxville, TN: University of Tennessee Value Added Research and Assessment Center.

Scherer, M. (2004, March). Perspectives: What works in reading? *Educational Leadership, 61*(6), 5.

Schlechty, P. (2001). *Shaking up the schoolhouse.* San Francisco: Jossey-Bass.

Schlechty, P. (2005). *Creating great schools: Six critical systems at the heart of educational innovation.* San Francisco: Jossey-Bass.

Schmoker, M. (1997). Setting goals in turbulent times. In A. Hargreaves (Ed.), *Rethinking educational change with the heart and mind: 1997 ASCD yearbook.* Alexandria, VA: Association for Supervision and Curriculum Development.

Schmoker, M. (1999). *Results: The key to continuous school improvement* (2nd ed.). Alexandria, VA: Association for Supervision and Curriculum Development.

Schmoker, M. (2001). The results fieldbook: Practical strategies from dramatically improved schools. *Journal of Staff Development, 23*(2), 10–13.

Schmoker, M. (2002, Spring). Up and away: Lifting low performance. *Journal of Staff Development, 23*(2), 10–13.

Schmoker, M. (2004, February). Tipping point: From feckless reform to substantive instructional improvement. *Phi Delta Kappan, 85*(6), 424–432.

Sharp, L., & Frechtling, J. (Eds.). (1997, August). *User-friendly handbook for mixed method evaluations.* Retrieved June 1, 2005 from www.nsf.gov/pubs/1997/nsf97153/start.htm

Showers, B. (1996). The evolution of peer coaching. *Educational Leadership, 53*(6), 12–16.

Silver, H. F., Strong, R. W., & Perini, M. J. (2000). *So each may learn: Integrating learning styles and multiple intelligences.* Alexandria, VA: Association for Supervision and Curriculum Development.

Skowron, J. (2001). *Powerful lesson planning models: The art of 1000 decisions.* Thousand Oaks, CA: Corwin Press.

Snow, D. (2003). *Classroom strategies for helping at-risk students: Noteworthy perspectives.* (revised ed.). Aurora, CO: Mid-continent Research for Education and Learning.

Solomon, P. G. (2003). *The curriculum bridge: From standards to actual classroom practice.* (2nd ed.). Thousand Oaks, CA: Corwin Press.

Sousa, D. A. (2001). *How the brain learns* (2nd ed.). Thousand Oaks, CA: Corwin Press.

Sparks, D. (1992). Merging content knowledge and pedagogy: An interview with Lee Shulman. *Journal of Staff Development, 13*(1). Retrieved January 15, 2005 from www.nedc.org/library/publications/jsd/shulman131.cfm

Sparks, D. (1996, February). Viewing reform from a systems perspective. *The Developer,* February 1996. (2, 6).

Sparks, D. (1999). Assessment without victims: Interview with Rick Stiggins. *Journal of Staff Development, 20*(2), 54–56.

Sparks, D. (2002). *Designing powerful professional development for teachers and principals.* Oxford, OH: National Staff Development Council.

Sparks, D. (2004a). *Leading for results.* Thousand Oaks, CA: Corwin Press.

Sparks, D. (2004b, Spring). Broader purpose calls for higher understanding: Interview with Andy Hargreaves. *Journal of Staff Development, 25*(2), 46–50.

Sparks, D. (2005a, April). Principals serve schools as leaders of professional learning. *Results,* (2).

Sparks, D. (2005b). Principals amplify teachers' outstanding practices. In D. Sparks (Ed.), *Leading for results: Transforming teaching, learning, and relationships in schools.* Alexandria, VA: National Staff Development Council.

Sparks, D. (2005c). *Transforming teaching, learning, and relationships in schools.* Thousand Oaks, CA: Corwin Press.

Sparks, D., & Hirsch, S. (1997). *A new vision for staff development.* Alexandria, VA: Association for Supervision and Curriculum Development and National Staff Development Council.

Sparks, D., & Loucks-Horsley, S. (1989). Five models of staff development for teachers. *Journal of Staff Development, 10*(4), 40–57.

Squires, D. A. (2005). *Aligning and balancing the standards-based curriculum.* Thousand Oaks, CA: Corwin Press.

Stein, M. L. (1993). *The beginning reading instruction study.* Washington, DC: US Government Printing Office.

Stiggins, R. J. (1999). Assessment, student confidence, and school success. *Phi Delta Kappan, 81*(3), 191–198.

Stiggins, R. J. (2000). *Student-involved classroom assessment* (3rd ed.). Englewood Cliffs, NJ: Prentice Hall.

Stigler, J. W., & Hiebert, J. (1999). *The teaching gap: Best ideas from the world's teachers for improving education in the classroom.* New York: The Free Press.

Strong, R. W., Silver, H. E., & Perini, M. J. (2001). *Teaching what matters most: Standards for raising student achievement.* Alexandria, VA: Association for Supervision and Curriculum Development.

Stronge, J. H. (2002). *Qualities of effective teachers.* Alexandria, VA: Association for Supervision and Curriculum Development.

Sylwester, R. (2000). *A biological brain in a cultural classroom.* Thousand Oaks, CA: Corwin Press.

Taggart, G. L., & Wilson, A. P. (1998). *Promoting reflective thinking in teachers: 44 action strategies.* Thousand Oaks, CA: Corwin Press.

Taylor, B. M., Pearson, P. D., Clark, K., & Walpole, S. (2000). Effective schools and accomplished teachers: Lessons about primary grade reading instruction in low income schools. *Elementary School Journal, 101,* 121–165.

Thompson, M. (2005). *Learning-focused strategies notebook.* Boone, NC: Learning Focused Solutions.

Thompson, M., & Thomason, J. (1998). *Increasing student performance and achievement: The learning-focused elementary schools.* VII (6), Video Program E, Part One & Part Two. Sandy, UT: The Video Journal of Education.

Thompson, M., Thomason, J., & Thompson, S. (2002). *Catching kids up: Learning-focused strategies for acceleration.* Boone, NC: Learning Concepts, Inc.

Tileston, D. W. (2000). *10 best teaching practices: Brain research, learning styles, and standards define teaching competencies.* Thousand Oaks, CA: Corwin Press.

Tomlinson, C. A. (1999). *The differentiated classroom: Responding to the needs of all learners.* Alexandria, VA: Association for Supervision and Curriculum Development.

Tucker, P. D., & Stronge, J. H. (2005). *Linking: Teacher evaluation and student achievement.* Alexandria, VA: Association for Supervision and Curriculum Development.

Tushnet, N. C., et al. (2004). *Longitudinal assessment of comprehensive school reform implementation and outcomes: First-year report.* Los Alamitos, CA: West Ed. Prepared for the U.S. Department of Education, Policy and Program Studies Service.

Vacca, R. T., & Vacca, J. L. (2002). *Content area reading: Literacy and learning across the curriculum* (7th ed.). Boston: Allyn & Bacon.

Wang, M. C., Reynolds, M. C., & Walberg, H. J. (1994 December/1995 January). Serving students at the margins. *Educational Leadership, 52*(4), 12–17.

Warren, R. (2002). *The purpose-driven life.* Grand Rapids, MI: Zondervan.

Wheatley, M. J., & Kellner-Rogers, M. (1996, July/August). *The irresistible future of organizing.* Retrieved May 30, 2005 from http://www.margaretwheatley.com/articles/irresistiblefuture/html

Wiggins, G. (1998). *Educative assessment: Designing assessments to inform and improve student performance.* San Francisco: Jossey-Bass.

Wiggins, G., & McTighe, J. (1998). *Understanding by design.* Alexandria, VA: Association for Supervision and Curriculum Development.

Wiggins, G., & McTighe, J. (2000). *Understanding by design: Study guide.* Alexandria, VA: Association for Supervision and Curriculum Development.

W. K. Kellogg Foundation. (1998, January). *Evaluation handbook.* Battle Creek, MI: Author.

W. K. Kellogg Foundation. (2001, December). *Logic model development guide.* Battle Creek, MI: Author, Item #1209. Retrieved May 21, 2005 from www.wkkf.org

Williams, B. (2004). *Closing the achievement gap: A vision for changing beliefs and practices* (2nd ed.). Alexandria, VA: Association for Supervision and Curriculum Development.

Williams, B., & Newcombe, E. (1994). Building on the strengths of urban learners. *Educational Leadership, 51*(8), 75–78.

Winfield, L. F. (1986). Teacher beliefs toward academically at-risk students in inner city urban schools. *Urban Review, 18,* 253–268.

Wolfe, P., & Nevills, P. (2004). *Building the reading brain, pre k–3.* Thousand Oaks, CA: Corwin Press.

York-Barr, J., Sommers, W. A., Ghere, G. S., & Montie, J. (2001). *Reflective practice to improve schools: An action guide for educators.* Thousand Oaks, CA: Corwin Press.

Zachary, L. J. (2005, January). Hold people accountable: Monitor progress and measure results. *Executive Excellence, 22*(1), 18.

Zemke, R. (1998). How to do a needs assessment when you think you don't have time. *Training, 35*(3), 38–44.

Zepeda, S. J. (1999). Arrange time into blocks. *Journal of Staff Development, 20*(2), 26–30.

Index

CORWIN PRESS